MAKERS
AND TAKERS

Also by Peter Schweizer

Do As I Say (Not As I Do): Profiles in Liberal Hypocrisy

Chain of Command (with Caspar Weinberger)

The Bushes: Portrait of a Dynasty
(with Rochelle Schweizer)

*Reagan's War: The Epic Story of His Forty-Year
Struggle and Final Triumph over Communism*

*The Fall of the Berlin Wall: Reassessing the Causes and
Consequences of the End of the Cold War*

The Next War (with Caspar Weinberger)

Disney: The Mouse Betrayed
(with Rochelle Schweizer)

*Victory: The Reagan Administration's Secret Strategy
that Hastened the Collapse of the Soviet Union*

*Friendly Spies: How America's Allies Are Using
Economic Espionage to Steal Our Secrets*

MAKERS AND TAKERS

Why Conservatives Work Harder, Feel Happier,
Have Closer Families, Take Fewer Drugs,
Give More Generously, Value Honesty More,
Are Less Materialistic and Envious, Whine Less . . .
and Even Hug Their Children More Than Liberals

Peter Schweizer

DOUBLEDAY

New York London Toronto Sydney Auckland

QD
DOUBLEDAY

Copyright © 2008 by Peter Schweizer

All Rights Reserved

Published in the United States by Doubleday, an imprint of The Doubleday Publishing Group, a division of Random House, Inc., New York.
www.doubleday.com

DOUBLEDAY is a registered trademark and the DD colophon is a trademark of Random House, Inc.

Book design by Nicola Ferguson

Library of Congress Cataloging-in-Publication Data
Schweizer, Peter, 1964–
    Makers and takers : why conservatives work harder, feel happier, have closer families, take fewer drugs, give more generously, value honesty more, are less materialistic and envious, whine less . . . and even hug their children more than liberals / Peter Schweizer. — 1st ed.
        p.   cm.
    Includes bibliographical references and index.
    1. United States—Politics and government—2001–2. 2. Liberalism—United States—History—21st century. 3. Conservatism—United States—History—21st century. 4. Right and left (Political science)—United States—History—21st century. I. Title.
    JK275.S38 2008
    320.50973—dc22   2008007672

ISBN 978-0-385-51350-0

PRINTED IN THE UNITED STATES OF AMERICA

10 9 8 7 6 5 4 3 2 1

First Edition

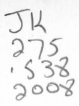

To the memory of Caspar W. Weinberger,
friend, mentor, patriot, gentleman

CONTENTS

Acknowledgments   ix

Introduction: *Why Conservatives and Liberals Are Different*   1

1. The Mighty Me: *Or, Why Liberals Are More Self-Centered Than Conservatives*   29

2. Think Globally, Sit on Your Butt Locally: *Or, Why Conservatives Are Actually More Generous Than Liberals*   55

3. Liberal\$ and Money: *Or, Why Liberals Are More Envious and Less Hardworking Than Conservatives*   81

4. The Whole Truth and Nothing But: *Or, Why Conservatives Value Honesty More Than Liberals*   105

5. Anger Management: *How Modern Liberalism Promotes Anger*   *133*

6. Mind Wars: *Why Conservatives Actually Know More Than Liberals*   *157*

7. Whine Country: *Or, Why Liberals Complain More*   *183*

Conclusion: *Why Did I Write This Book?*   *209*

Notes   *213*

Index   *249*

ACKNOWLEDGMENTS

I have been affiliated with the Hoover Institution on War, Revolution and Peace as a research fellow since 1999. It is hard to find a better intellectual environment in which to work. Given that I first became interested in political ideas reading Milton Friedman and Thomas Sowell in high school, walking the halls of the Hoover Institution has been a truly inspirational experience. I'm still every bit as fascinated by the ideas being generated by my Hoover colleagues as I was back in high school.

John Raisian has given me support and the opportunity to write and think about ideas that I care about, sometimes even if they move in difficult directions. John, thanks for your leadership and friendship. Thanks also to David Brady, Richard Sousa, Stephen Langlois, Jeff Bliss, Don Meyer, and Noel Kolak for their faithful leadership and encouragement. I would also like to thank the following individuals who have either directly or indirectly inspired me over the years with their ideas and commitment to scholarship: Richard V. Allen, George Shultz, Peter Berkowitz, Martin Anderson, Ken Jowitt, Tom Henriksen, Michael McFaul, Thomas Sowell, Edwin Meese, Victor Davis Hanson, Tod Lindberg, Kiron Skinner, and Robert Zelnick. I also want to say a special thanks to my good friend, Hoover fellow Peter Robinson. Thanks for your wisdom, remarkable spirit, and friendship.

A number of friends have inspired me over the years and I am truly grateful. Thanks to Ron Robinson at Young America's Foundation: It was Ron who first introduced me to the writings of Milton Friedman, Thomas Sowell, and so many others. Fellow writers and friends Wynton Hall, David Ridenour, John Bickley, Paul Kengor, Bill Mattox, Chris Ruddy, and Bob McClure also encouraged me and helped to pick me up when I was feeling down. I also want to thank Stephen K. Bannon: Your passion is infectious.

Thanks also to everyone at Doubleday, who were supportive of this project from the beginning: Stephen Rubin, Bill Thomas, Nicole Dewey, and Dan Feder. I am deeply indebted to my editor, Adam Bellow, one of the most original thinkers I have met in my life. Thanks, my good friend, for all of your insight and help.

Finally, what can I say about my family? They are patient when I'm up late working on the manuscript and encouraging when I've had enough and about to throw the laptop into the pool. My dearest Rochelle, thanks for sticking with me.

Jack and Hannah, thank you for being our children. You are the best thing that has ever happened to us. To my mom, Kerstin Schweizer, thanks for the encouraging words every time we speak. Joe, Maria, Rich, and Evelyn, thanks for putting up with me.

This book is dedicated to the memory of the late Caspar Weinberger, who I had the good fortune to know, and to work with, for fifteen years. He was a friend, mentor, patriot, and gentleman. R.I.P., Cap.

MAKERS
AND TAKERS

INTRODUCTION
Why Conservatives and Liberals Are Different

"All people are born alike," Groucho Marx once said. "Except Republicans and Democrats."

Groucho might have been joking, but today the differences between liberals and conservatives are widely discussed and debated. And somehow, they always break to the advantage of the left. What's more, it's not conservative ideas that are under assault, but conservatives themselves. Conservatives are said to suffer from severe personality defects and a host of other maladies that make them dysfunctional—if not actually dangerous.

George Lakoff, a professor of linguistics at the University of California at Berkeley (where else?), has a popular theory. Embracing the "unimpeded pursuit of self-interest," conservatives will do pretty much anything to get what they want. Lakoff has nightmares because conservatives are "mean and greedy," and "what is even scarier is that they believe" what they say. On top of which, they are abusive to their kids. They ignore their children when they cry and are instead busy "beating them with sticks, belts, and paddles," he writes.[1]

"Unlike conservatives, [Democrats] believe in working for the public good and social justice," Lakoff explains without presenting a shred of evidence. But he doesn't lay out these theories in books released by fringe publishers. These ideas come from his book *Moral Politics,* released by the University of Chicago Press. What explains this horrid emotional and psychological wasteland that is the modern conservative? Lakoff (who is not a psychologist) speculates that conservatives are the product of bad parenting. Raised in a "strict father" home, they are emotionally warped and wounded, and this explains why they are apparently prone to anger and violence. Lakoff warns, "The more children brought up with strict father values, the more conservatives we will have." That this is a very bad thing apparently needs no argumentation.

Liberals, on the other hand, are products of a "nurturing home," and that's why they are so generous and caring. A true liberal, Lakoff writes, "is empathetic; helps the disadvantaged, protects those who need protection, promotes and exemplifies fulfillment in life, and takes care of himself so he can do all this."

Lakoff is no isolated crank. Howard Dean, chairman of the Democratic National Committee, has hailed him as "one of the most influential political thinkers of the progressive movement" and made his book required reading for his staff. Democratic senators have invited him to speak at private retreats, and he was considered "an unofficial aide-de-camp" to the Kerry campaign. His ideas get regular play on PBS and NPR, and his books are assigned in dozens of college classrooms.

Other academics have made similar "scientific" claims. In March 2006, a pair of professors from UC-Berkeley *(quelle coincidence!)* published a paper in the *Journal of Research in Personality* which explained that insecure, whiny children grow up to be conservatives. The article was immediately picked up by major news outfits like the *Chicago Sun-Times* and Canada's *Toronto Star.* "Remember the whiny, insecure kid in nursery school, the one who always thought everyone was out to get him, and was always running to the teacher with complaints? Chances are he grew up to be a conservative," noted the *Sun-Times.* "The confident kids turned out liberal and were still hanging loose, turning into bright, non-conforming adults with wide interests. [The study] reasons that insecure kids look for reassurance provided by tradition and authority, and find it in conservative politics."[2]

Never mind that this "study" was based entirely on the subjective observations of two admittedly liberal researchers.

The finding was embraced by news outlets around the world because it conformed to the media image of conservatives as being psychologically deformed.

Another group of professors from (you guessed it) UC-Berkeley, the University of Maryland, and Stanford University claimed in another study that conservatives are emotionally unstable: motivated by "fear and aggression," prone to "dogmatism," they struggle with "terror management" and are subject to "uncertainty avoidance." (Given all of this, why would you want to be a conservative—or even live near one?) The authors claimed in the American Psychological Association's *Psychological Bulletin* that conservatives support such things as (are you ready?) the Indian caste system and apartheid in South Africa because they are afraid of change.

Naturally, conservatives are not as "integratively complex" as liberals (can you say simpleminded?), and are prone to embrace "simplistic clichés and stereotypes." Apparently Homer Simpson votes Republican. Talk show host Rush Limbaugh and former President Ronald Reagan think a lot like Hitler and Mussolini, these academics assure us, because they all preach "a return to an idealized past" and condone inequality. The researchers reveal their own bizarre political views when they include both Joseph Stalin and Fidel Castro as "politically conservative" leaders. Evidently, because communists are resistant to giving up political power, that makes them conservatives.[3]

How did they reach this scientific conclusion? By looking at politicians' speeches, other research articles (no bias there, of course), and verdicts rendered by judges. Despite the clear ideological agenda couched in academic language, the study found its way into dozens of publications, including the *San Francisco Chronicle* and the *New York Times*. The study, by the way, was funded by federal grants.

A growing number of academics have also embraced this view. Conservatives are selfish, says Robert Reich, once Bill Clinton's secretary of labor and now a professor at Berkeley (where else?), and they "pander to the worst in us." The late John Kenneth Galbraith, professor at Harvard and don of liberal economists, once said that conservatives are simply in search of "a superior moral justification for selfishness."[4] Karen Stenner, a professor at Princeton, argues that conservatives are authoritarian, punitive, and prone to dictatorial tendencies.[5] Another group of scholars describes conservatives as "pinched and neurotic."[6]

Academics clearly have it in for conservatives. In 2004 the Center for Survey Research & Analysis at the University of Connecticut conducted a survey among college seniors at America's top fifty colleges and universities (as reported by *U.S. News & World Report*); 47 percent reported that their professors made negative comments about conservatives. Only 15 percent said professors made negative comments about liberals.[7] The media is so hungry for these stories that when hoaxes on the Internet claimed to prove that liberals are more intelligent than conservatives, major news outlets picked the stories up, accepting them uncritically.

Beyond the academic world, there are plenty who embrace the idea that the problem is not just conservative ideas, but conservatives themselves. Stephen Ducat, a San Francisco Bay–area psychologist, argued in *The Wimp Factor* that there is a link between "the magnitude of a man's femiphobia and his tendency to embrace right-wing political opinions." In other words, conservatives are sexually repressed prudes with lots of hang-ups. Needless to say, *Publishers Weekly* praised the book for its "fresh and complex insights," and it enjoyed favorable coverage in the *San Francisco Chronicle, Los Angeles Times,* and *Psychology Today.* Naturally, it's been quoted on popular lefty websites like Daily Kos, Think Progress, and Common Dreams. It has even been assigned in classes at Brandeis and Amherst, among other places. Robert Kuttner, coeditor of the generally serious *American Prospect,* shares this view. In an article titled "The Politics of Family," Kuttner wrote, "It's the right that battles repressed demons often with violent or kinky results."[8]

Others have attacked conservatives for what they see as serious character flaws. John Dean, once Richard Nixon's attorney, has written several angry books aimed at conservatives. In *Conservatives Without a Conscience,* Dean explains that political conservatives are "arrogant, condescending, and self-righteous." Elsewhere he adds that they are "moralistic" and "negative." Dean further contends that conservatives have "little facility for self-analysis" and a "disposition to dominate others."

Many in the media agree. The prestigious review organ *Booklist* proclaimed, "Readers of all political perspectives will find this book riveting." When Dean appeared on CNN to discuss the book, he noted that conservatives have "that type of personality that really doesn't like self-criticism; it doesn't want to hear the other side of an argument." That comment—and many others like it—went unchallenged, despite overwhelming evidence that (these days at least) the description applies more accurately to liberals, especially on college campuses. Or indeed, to Dean himself. When Dean appeared on *The Daily Show* with Jon Stewart, he was greeted with softball questions, and praise from Stewart about his "scientific approach." On the MSNBC program *Countdown*, host Keith Olbermann could only nod in agreement as Dean laid out his thesis.

Rank-and-file liberals ate it up: The book spent six weeks on the *New York Times* bestseller list.

Dean is not alone in advancing the thesis that conservatives are ignorant, dangerous, and more than a little bit weird. Jim Weaver, a former congressman from Oregon (and apparently an amateur geneticist), argues in *Two Kinds: The Genetic Origins of Conservative and Liberal* that conservatives have personality disorders that make them "aggressive attackers and acquirers" who are also "insensitive to the plight of others." Liberals on the other hand are "more imaginative and thoughtful." Instead of attacking, as conservatives are prone to do, liberals are "cooperative." He concludes by invoking the biblical story of Cain and Abel. It's not too often you hear a liberal quote the Bible. But the congressman adds a modern-day twist. Conservatives are like Cain, the selfish brother, unconcerned with others and willing to kill for what they want. Liberals are like Abel, always trying to do the right thing.

Sen. Barbara Boxer, in her forgettable novel *A Time to Run*, offered up a political thriller that spelled out her theory of how nutty and emotionally wounded conservatives are. The novel's heroes are a pair of California liberals, Josh and Ellen, described by a *Los Angeles Times* reporter as "liberal, altruistic, sane." The lone conservative in the book is Greg, from dreary Ohio. Unlike the happy (and tanned) Josh and Ellen, Greg likes beer, football, and hunting. (These are supposed to be danger signs.) In the end, Greg marries a wealthy socialite and lives off her money. But it isn't really his fault: We soon learn that he was raised by an "emotionally abusive" father. As Senator Boxer explained in an interview, the novel explores "why people become liberals and conservatives," and demonstrates how "the fact that [liberals] had loving families made a big difference."[9]

This is what liberals say when they are being polite. Garrison Keillor pulls no punches when he rants in a left-wing magazine that Republicans are "swamp developers and corporate shills, faith-based economists, fundamentalist bullies with Bibles, Christians of convenience, freelance racists, misanthropic frat boys, shrieking midgets of AM radio, tax cheats, nihilists in golf pants, brownshirts in pinstripes, sweatshop tycoons, hacks, aggressive dorks. . . . " He goes on, but you get the idea.[10]

Democratic Party chairman Howard Dean covers all the bases, telling Americans that conservatives and Republicans are "evil," "corrupt," "brain-dead," and for good measure "not nice people" who "have never made an honest living in their lives," "are not friendly to different kinds of people," and "always divide people."

Bring enough conservatives together and you get what many on the left consider hell on earth. James Wolcott, former editor of *Vanity Fair* and now a cantankerous liberal blogger, has written that "the Red states spread like a blood stain across America's outstretched body." Hollywood is currently producing a movie called *Red State*, which is, naturally, a horror film. "It's very much about that subject matter," says director Kevin Smith, "that point of view and that position taken to absolute extreme."

"You see the state where James Byrd was lynch-dragged behind a pickup truck until his body came apart—it's red," wrote Clinton adviser Paul Begala. "You see where Matthew Shepard was crucified on a split-rail fence for the crime of being gay—it's red. You see the state where right-wing extremists blew up a federal office building and murdered scores of federal employees: red. The state where an Army private thought to be gay was bludgeoned to death with a baseball bat, and the state where neo-Nazi skinheads murdered two African Americans because of their skin color, and the state where Bob Jones University spews its anti-Catholic bigotry: They're red too."[11] I don't really want to quibble—these are terrible events—but does anyone doubt that a similar list of appalling crimes could be compiled in the blue states of California, Massachusetts, and New York?

William O'Rourke, a columnist for the *Chicago Sun-Times*, explains that red America is "filled with vestiges of gun-loving, Ku-Klux-Klan sponsoring, formerly lynching-happy, survivalist-minded, hate-crime-perpetrating, non-blue-blooded, rugged individualists . . . which contains not one primary center of intellectual or creative density."[12]

Populated by emotionally damaged individuals with deep character flaws, it's no wonder that the red states are such horrible places to live. Wolcott paints a picture of life in the red states as a living hell, citing all sorts of statistics to make his case. Nine out of the ten states with the highest rates of incarceration, fourteen of the fifteen with the highest suicide rates, and nine of the top ten in illegitimate births are red states, he explains. Others paint the red states as being populated by ignorant boobs.

Many of these statistics are skewed. But this sort of simplistic approach is ridiculous on its face. No state is completely "red" or "blue." In predominantly blue California, there are millions of conservatives. Bush won 45 percent of the vote in 2004 and received more than five and a half million votes. In red state Arkansas, John Kerry managed 45 percent and received only one hundred thousand fewer votes than Bush. You simply can't lump millions of people together into "red" or "blue" and draw much of a conclusion. Had Wolcott done even the most basic research, he would have discovered, for example, that in a red state like South Dakota, the suicide rate is highest in *blue* counties, while births to unwed mothers in a red state like Alabama are higher in heavily Democratic counties.

But the liberal prejudice against conservatives is firm and deeply rooted. David Early, a reporter for the *San Jose Mercury News,* openly "wondered how anyone he liked or admired could be a Republican."[13] Novelist Kurt Vonnegut said: "What are conservatives? They are people who will move heaven and earth, if they have to, who will ruin a company or a country or a planet, to prove to us and to themselves that they are superior to everyone else. . . . Conservatives are crazy as bedbugs. They are bullies."[14]

Even a relatively apolitical humorist like Dave Barry buys into this prejudice, noting that liberal Democrats "seem to be basically nicer people" than conservative Republicans. One slogan that liberals can buy on a T-shirt or refrigerator magnet reads, "Republicans are people, too. Mean, selfish, greedy people."

All sorts of defects are assigned to conservatives. Columnist Michael Kinsley says that conservatives are "arrogant" and dumb, as opposed to liberals who are "crippled by reason and open-mindedness." Novelist Jane Smiley explains that George W. Bush won the presidency by "exploiting ignorance in the citizenry. . . . Ignorance and bloodlust have a long tradition in the United States, especially in the red states. . . . The history of the last four years shows that red state types, above all, do not want to be told what to do—they prefer to be ignorant. As a result, they are virtually unteachable."[15] Journalist Bill Moyers fears that the republic is in danger because conservatives are "oblivious to the facts," by which, of course, he means *his* facts. The late Bella Abzug called conservatives "know nothings," and cartoonist Ted Rall reasons that the red states are a vast expanse of ignorance because, after all, "the best and the brightest gravitate to places where liberalism rules."

Frank Rich of the *New York Times* says that conservatives live in "perpetual fear," anxious and paranoid about everything. (Obviously the left is not driven by fear—fear of global warming, fear of nuclear winter, or fear of a fascist coup by George W. Bush.) This charge is nothing new. Political scientist Richard Hofstadter explained fifty years ago that conservatives responded to a "paranoid style" of politics while liberals were more rational. In his classic book *Anti-Intellectualism in American Life,* Hofstadter argued that liberals were rational but faced resistance from ignorant conservatives. Another academic, writing in the *American Political Science Review,* explained quite bluntly that "conservative beliefs are found most frequently among the uninformed, the poorly educated, and, so far as we can determine, the less intelligent." He also noted that "conservatism, in our society at least, appears to be far more characteristic of social isolates, of people who think poorly of themselves, who suffer personal disgruntlement and frustration, who are submissive, timid, and wanting in confidence, etc." On the other hand, "the most articulate and informed classes in our society are preponderantly liberal in their outlook."[16]

Hollywood also plays up the idea that the world is populated by dysfunctional conservatives and brilliant, well-adjusted liberals. According to a group of academics who examined 124 political characters in 47 popular films spanning five decades, liberal characters tended to be "depicted as more intelligent, friendly, and good" than conservatives. They were also (big surprise) more physically attractive.[17]

So the cultural cues are out there and reinforce the liberal bias that those on the left are the best people: the most intelligent, the best informed, the most public spirited, and the most morally pure.[18]

Individual conservatives face this ridiculous stereotype all the time. Over the years, conservative Republican presidents have been attacked not just for being wrong, but also for being mentally unstable. During the 1964 presidential election, Hofstadter famously explained that Senator Goldwater and his followers were paranoid. Journalist Ralph Ginsberg, publisher of *Fact* magazine, ran a lengthy article called "The Mind of Barry Goldwater." He quoted several shrinks who declared that the Arizona Republican was certifiably crazy. Ronald Reagan was the inhabitant of a mental Disneyland, caused by his father's alcoholism (or so says Garry Wills). And George W. Bush? He has, to use the technical term, "lost his mind," according to *New York* magazine: "Bush suffers from a classic case of Narcissistic Personality Disorder."[19]

When things go terribly wrong in America, it is usually a result of a conservative character flaw. As James Piereson points out in *Camelot and the Cultural Revolution,* when

John F. Kennedy was assassinated, many in the media were quick to blame conservatives even though the gunman, Lee Harvey Oswald, was a card-carrying communist. Columnist Drew Pearson blamed hatred emanating from the right wing. Grayson Kirk, president of Columbia University at the time, called for a crackdown on the radical right. It was left to Arthur Krock of the *New York Times* to point out that Lee Harvey Oswald was a committed Marxist who had defected to the Soviet Union. But those details were apparently unimportant.[20]

It's not simply conservative policies that are wrong. The problem is that conservatives suffer from a deficient moral code, and concomitant character flaws. Conservatives are backward, ignorant, and selfish. Liberals on the other hand are enlightened, just, fair, emotionally mature, stable, and calm. Cartoonist Ted Rall captured this liberal smugness perfectly after the 2004 election: "So our guy lost the election. Why shouldn't those of us on the coasts feel superior? We eat better, travel more, dress better, watch cooler movies, earn better salaries, meet more interesting people, listen to better music, and know more about what's going on in the world. If you voted for Bush, we accept that we have to share the country with you. We're adjusting to the possibility that there may be more of you than there are of us. But don't demand our respect."[21]

Why paint conservatives as nuts? Aside from scoring political points and encouraging a sense of moral superiority, it allows those on the left to avoid debating or even listening to conservatives. Why listen to the ravings of a lunatic? Brian Anderson reports on a recent seminar that included liberal philosophy professors who were discussing how to deal with conflicts over abortion, homosexuality, and pornography. When one professor argued that in a free society these issues should be debated openly between liberals and conservatives, another dismissed him. "Why should we listen to loons?" he asked.

This has become the preferred tactic of the left. Rather than discuss conservative ideas, the left dismisses them on the grounds that conservatives are so messed up one shouldn't waste the time.[22]

The ridiculous liberal caricature laid out above in overwhelming detail is simply not supported by the evidence. (As we shall see, often the exact opposite is true.) But these liberal/left attacks do contain a kernel of truth: Liberals and conservatives are different. They have very different worldviews, lifestyles, and tendencies. There are real consistent differences between them. Some of those differences are quirky and fun. Scarborough Research, a New York City–based consumer research service, has discovered that conservatives tend to water-ski, hunt, garden, and play musical instruments in far higher numbers than liberals. Those on the left are more prone to watch TV, visit an art museum, gamble, or go dancing in a club.

Other marketing firms have found that liberals and conservatives tend to make dramatically different consumer choices. Conservatives count beef as their favorite meat while liberals tend to prefer chicken. Conservatives buy Porsches in overwhelming numbers while liberals skew heavily toward Volvos. (What this means is anyone's guess. Perhaps conservatives are looking for speed while liberals are bracing themselves for the next accident.)

On television, advertisers have discovered that conservatives watch *JAG, Law & Order,* and football while liberals tune in to *Judging Amy, Will & Grace,* and, for some reason, *Judge Judy.* At the movies, liberals like films about politicians and lawyers (think *Erin Brockovich*), while conservatives prefer films about soldiers and cops.[23]

How do we know about these differences? Because a wide array of research has taken place in recent years that looks at how people think and live, what they buy, watch, and eat, even the moral choices they make. What the research shows is that conservatives and liberals have very different tendencies.

Does this mean that all conservatives hate cats, or that none of them watched and enjoyed *Erin Brockovich?* Does it mean that there are no liberals out there who hate abstract art? Of course not. I tend to be politically conservative and yet I drive a Volvo. What we are talking about are *tendencies and preferences that are not always correct* but nonetheless largely reflect the realities of modern American life.

We know these different tendencies exist because in a large number of studies and scientific surveys, liberals and conservatives tell us they exist. These differences go beyond the seemingly unimportant consumer decisions people make.

Perhaps the biggest divide between liberals and conservatives today is not their consumer preferences or even how they vote, but the underlying values by which they live their lives.

Some of these differences we recognize intuitively, even absent supporting research. Consider the manner in which conservatives and liberals express themselves. If you are watching a protest march, you can quickly figure out whether the protesters are liberals or conservatives—even if you don't look at the signs. The way they dress, walk, and handle themselves often give us sufficient clues. One protest in Washington, D.C., was recently attended by tens of thousands of people and included drumming workshops, puppet shows, and poetry readings. I don't need to tell you that this protest was organized by the political left. When was the last time you saw conservatives holding puppets at a protest rally? (Not that there's anything wrong with that!)

It is my contention that liberalism and conservatism are not simply political ideologies, but represent divergent ways of life. For those on both sides, their political views are just the tip of an encompassing worldview that addresses the biggest questions about life. This worldview influences the decisions they make about family, work, community, and life.

Imagine for a moment that you are at a dinner party and the woman next to you is wearing a multicolored skirt, Birkenstocks, large rustic jewelry, and no makeup. If she tells you she's pro-choice, it's a good bet she is also opposed to drilling for oil in Alaska, against Bush's tax cuts, and has certain predictable views about religion. It's also safe to assume she doesn't drive a Hummer. On the other hand, if you meet someone in a suit who just came from a Bible study group, it is a fair bet that this person is conservative. This person is probably not a vegan, is married or wants to get married, and believes in capitalism.

Professor Bruce Fleming is an avowed liberal who teaches at the conservative U.S. Naval Academy and has observed the distinctive differences between liberals and conservatives over many years. As he puts it, both liberals and conservatives have "structural patterns" in their lives; in other words, "liberalism and conservatism aren't merely lists of disparate beliefs, but configurations of beliefs radiating outward from a center. Liberalism is not simply a set of political ideas, but is today a form of social identity."[24]

This sort of analysis is not particularly new. George Orwell noted in his book *The Road to Wigan Pier* that in postwar Britain, politics was closely related to social identity. He found this particularly true on the left. "One sometimes gets the impression that the mere words 'Socialism' and 'Communism' draw towards them with magnetic force every fruit-juice drinker, nudist, sandal-wearer, sex-maniac, Quaker, 'Nature Cure' quack, pacifist, and feminist in England," he wrote. Of course he didn't have the benefit of research to determine whether his observation was correct. But accurate or not, Orwell saw a link between the lifestyle choices people made and their political worldviews.

Today we have at our disposal something Orwell did not enjoy: an enormous wealth of research that allows us to track the differences between liberals and conservatives with a very fine degree of specificity. What that research shows is that conservatives and liberals are indeed very different from one another. But they are different in ways that many readers may find startling.

Much of this research, gathered from top-rated scientific institutions around the globe, has been completely ignored by the media and academic world for one very simple reason: It does not conform to their ideological stereotypes. Consider a simple example. It has long been assumed that anti-Semitism is a conservative vice that liberals, being the tolerant and open-minded sort, are less prone to embrace. Conservative Republicans are the ones who accept ugly stereotypes about Jews. Supporting evidence? Who needs it? This is just something "everyone" seems to "know." Sen. Chuck Schumer exemplified this attitude during an appearance on Bill Maher's HBO show *Real Time.* "There are some, you know there are some anti-Semites in this country, but most of them would vote Republican anyway," he declared. Naturally Bill Maher never challenged him, nor would any liberal news anchor on television today. It is widely assumed (even by many conservatives) that anti-Semites are red state Republicans. A survey by the Jerusalem Center for Public Affairs found that Jewish leaders *perceived Republicans* as being more anti-Semitic.[25] But has anyone actually checked the numbers?

The General Social Survey regularly asks thousands of Americans their attitudes on a host of issues. Conducted by the University of Chicago and the National Opinion Research Center, it is one of the most authoritative surveys in the world. A few years ago the survey asked Americans about Jewish stereotypes. Are Jews more violent? Are they more money driven? Do they have too much influence? Surprisingly, on every one of these questions, self-described liberals were much more likely to embrace the stereotype than conservatives. Twenty-three percent of those who called themselves "very liberal" agreed that Jews were prone to violence, compared with only 14 percent of those who were "very conservative." Run the numbers based on whether the respondents considered themselves Republican or Democrat and you get the same pattern: 18 percent of strong Democrats agreed with that statement, compared with only 9 percent of Republicans.

When it comes to the stereotype that Jews are inordinately rich and money driven, 45 percent of strong Democrats agreed with the statement compared with 36 percent of strong Republicans. The same numbers came up when the respondents described themselves as conservative or liberal.

The same sort of simple research reveals the ridiculous nature of the attacks on conservatives. Take Lakoff's contention about how nurturing and caring liberal parents are compared with those nasty conservatives. Had he done even basic research, he would have discovered that conservatives spend *more* time with their children than liberals and actually hug them more than liberals do. He would also have discovered that conservatives are much closer to their parents, and are more trusting of family members than those on the left.

As for the Berkeley studies claiming that whiners tend to be conservatives, had they simply looked at authoritative research on attitudes, they would have found that those on the political left are much more likely to complain about their jobs, their families, their neighbors, their health, and their relative wealth—even when they earn the same as conservatives. In short, the major surveys show that those on the left tend to be chronically dissatisfied with almost everything in their lives. In their attacks on conservatives as uncaring, ignorant, nasty, mean, greedy, angry, selfish, and lazy, liberals are certainly entitled to their opinions. But they are not entitled to their own set of facts.

The research is clear. Looking at data gathered by the most authoritative and reliable academic research centers in the country as well as academic studies published in refereed journals, a pattern emerged that has until now been completely ignored. When compared to conservatives on a long list of personality and moral traits, modern liberals consistently come up short.

Liberals are, in the aggregate:

. . . more selfish. Liberals are much more likely to
think about themselves first and less willing to make
sacrifices for others. They are less interested in caring for a physically ill or elderly family member, and

more concerned with ensuring that their own needs are being met.

. . . more focused on money. Liberals are much more likely to report that money is important to them, that they don't earn enough, and that money is what matters in a job. They are also more likely to be envious of others.

. . . less hardworking. When considering a new job, liberals are more interested in job security and vacation time than their conservative counterparts. They also tend to value hard work less and embrace leisure as more desirable. Conservatism on the other hand is directly associated with the so-called Protestant Ethic.

. . . less emotionally satisfied. Liberals are much more likely to suffer from a nervous breakdown, attempt suicide, suffer from depression, and be chronically angry.

. . . less honest. Liberals are more likely to believe that it's okay to be dishonest or deceptive, cheat on their taxes (and their spouse), keep money that doesn't belong to them, and sell a used car with a faulty transmission to a family member.

. . . less knowledgeable about civic affairs and economics. Despite claims that conservatives are ignorant, studies and surveys show that conservatives and

Republicans tend to know more about public affairs, have a better understanding of economics, and do better on word association tests.

We'll also discover compelling evidence that conservatives are, again in the aggregate:

. . . happier and better adjusted. Conservatives are more satisfied with their lives, their professions, and even their health, even when compared to liberals with the same demographics (age, income, etc.).

. . . generally more successful parents. Obviously there are many exceptions, but conservatives in general are more willing to make sacrifices for their children, and their children in turn are less likely to take drugs, smoke, or drink at a young age. Conservative families are also closer. They are more likely to stay in touch with each other on a regular basis and trust each other more.

. . . more generous. For all the talk of liberal compassion, the reality is that conservatives are much more likely to donate money and time to charitable causes. Also, the reasons that liberals and conservatives get involved in charities tend to be different. Liberals support charities to "make a statement." Conservatives want to improve the lives of the people they are trying to help.

. . . less angry. Conservatives are less likely to become angry at someone, less likely to seek revenge, and less likely to throw or break things in a temper.

Conservatives have long argued that liberal policies promote social decay—destroying the work ethic, promoting relativism, and undermining social values. In *Slouching Toward Gomorrah,* Judge Robert Bork pointed to a coarsening of American culture as the price of liberalism. Ronald Reagan campaigned on the notion that the modern welfare state was undermining the American work ethic. In his book *My Cold War,* Irving Kristol wrote about his movement from the political left to the right: "What began to concern me more and more were the clear signs of rot and decadence germinating within American society—a rot and decadence that were no longer the consequence of liberalism but was the actual agenda of contemporary liberalism. . . . Sector after sector of American life has been ruthlessly corrupted by the liberal ethos. It is an ethos that aims simultaneously at political and social collectivism on the one hand, and moral anarchy on the other." Free market economists like Milton Friedman have likewise argued that high taxation destroys the work ethic while encouraging a sense of dependence.

What I will show is that liberalism not only leads to social decay, but can also lead to personal decay. Richard Weaver once declared, in an oft-overused line, that "ideas have consequences." John Maynard Keynes, the economist and keen-eyed critic and social observer, understood this perfectly when he wrote: "The ideas of economists and political philosophers, both when they are right and wrong, are more powerful than commonly understood. Indeed the world is ruled by little else."

I will argue that liberalism promotes a way of thinking, a way of life, and a pattern of living that are destructive on many levels. It is easy to view political beliefs as just a bunch of words that have very little to do with everyday life. Even thoughtful conservative authors like David Brooks have emphasized the similarities between liberals and conservatives who may vote differently but send their kids to the same schools, watch the same TV shows, and drive the same SUVs. But what you believe influences how you behave and what you do. Ideas impact behavior, and bad ideas generate bad outcomes. What's more, bad ideas have consequences not simply for individuals, but for their communities and countries as a whole.

The liberal line of argument has been that conservatives possess serious flaws and embrace conservatism as a result of their personal defects. My contention, based on a wealth of research, is the opposite: Modern liberal ideas consistently encourage bad habits and destructive behavioral tendencies. For example, modern liberalism holds that truth is a relative thing, and that it is difficult to know what "reality" is. This belief, widely held on the left today, has, as we shall see, a very real and practical effect on how liberals view the need for honesty in both private and public affairs.

At an even more fundamental level, however, modern liberalism simply absolves its adherents of many difficult and inconvenient responsibilities. Modern liberals believe that it is the responsibility of government to meet the needs of those who are poor or ill. The result is that liberals are actually less charitable than conservatives and less directly and personally concerned with the plight of others. Because liberals believe it is the role of the state to care for the needy, liberalism fosters an "I gave at the office" mentality. Simply espousing liberal values and voting for liberal candidates is enough. No other action is required.

This is why liberalism is so seductive. It allows one to claim the moral high ground on just about any issue while in effect "outsourcing" your personal responsibility for doing something about it to the government.

It is my argument that liberalism encourages destructive attitudes that are paradoxical and seemingly contradictory. It actively encourages a victim mentality while sanctioning anger as a genuine and healthy emotion; it discourages hard work while at the same time promoting a fixation on money. Indeed, it is my contention that liberalism, far from being a victimless belief system, often damages its own adherents the most. Conservative ideas on the other hand promote virtues that make people happier, healthier, more productive, and better citizens.

Conservative ideas promote hard work, a family-centered orientation, generosity, honesty, and compassion for others—the kind of virtues that contribute to society. In short, conservatives are "makers." They are the people who build, run, and fix things; they make our society function. Liberalism, in contrast, discourages hard work, promotes a sense of entitlement, and often leads to chronic dissatisfaction and an "outsourcing" of one's moral obligations. In other words, liberalism promotes an attitude of "taking."

My evidence for these broad and bold assertions is drawn from a wide range of reputable scholarly sources, primarily opinion research surveys. And it is important to stress at the outset that these are aggregate findings. There will be many individual exceptions on both sides. No one should say (and I am not arguing) that all conservatives are clean, upstanding, moral citizens while all liberals are selfish, greedy, and angry. But the evidence does show quite clearly that there tend to be important distinctions between these groups.

It may also be objected that polls and attitude surveys are imperfect tools, and that the differences revealed here are simply a reflection of the fact that liberals are more honest in answering these questions. But there is simply no evidence to support this contention. It is, of course, very difficult to ascertain whether people are giving truthful answers. But validation studies on questions relating to voting or drug use have found that the groups most likely to misreport in such studies are blacks and Democrats.[26]

Also, keep in mind that we are talking here about the influence of ideas on the way we act and live. While few of us really live up to our principles, it is important that they retain moral authority in our eyes. For the values we exalt—or denigrate—do have a material effect on our behavior.

1

THE MIGHTY ME
Or, Why Liberals Are More
Self-Centered Than Conservatives

The archetype of the modern liberal is not John F. Kennedy, Franklin D. Roosevelt, Martin Luther King, Hubert Humphrey, or even Jimmy Carter. It is Peter Pan, the mythical character who avoids responsibility, refuses to grow up, and is terribly self-absorbed.

Ronald Reagan kept a plaque on his Oval Office desk that read: "There is no limit to what a man can do, if he doesn't care who gets the credit." Reagan often reflected this attitude. After he left the White House, the economy was strong, the Cold War was won, and national pride had been restored.

Dismissive of praise, he headed quietly back to California. "I'm not a great man," he would say. "I just believe in great ideas."

In contrast, Bill Clinton has spent his post–White House years giving speeches about what he accomplished as president. Even his closest friends recognize that he is obsessed with his favorite subject—himself. In an in-depth profile of Clinton in the usually friendly *Vanity Fair,* veteran journalist Robert Sam Anson explained the frustrations of his friends. "He just talks. You don't really have a conversation with him. . . . He is just self-absorbed. Totally." According to Anson, Clinton has "a hankering for attention that makes him a joke even to admirers." His 957-page memoir *My Life* has been called one of the most "self-absorbed" pieces of literature in American history.[1]

Clinton may seem to be an easy target. But he is not alone. He is in fact a perfect reflection of contemporary liberalism and its obsession with self, individual freedom, personal growth, and "doing what feels good." One of the central aims of modern liberalism is avoiding commitment and responsibilities by outsourcing them to the government. Autonomy and independence, avoiding constraints imposed by family, tradition, churches, and community are a major preoccupation. If you don't believe me, consider these results from the highly regarded General Social Survey:

Do you get happiness by putting someone else's happiness ahead of your own? Of those who described themselves as "very conservative," 55 percent said yes. Those who described themselves as "very liberal"? Only 20 percent agreed.

Would you endure all things for the one you love? More than half—55 percent of conservatives—said yes, compared with only 26 percent of liberals.

Are you willing to sacrifice your wishes to let the one you love succeed? Only 33 percent of liberals said yes, compared with 57 percent of conservatives.

Is it your obligation to care for a seriously injured/ill spouse or parent, or should you give care only if you really want to? Fully 71 percent of conservatives said it was. Less than half (46 percent) of liberals agreed.[2]

Today's liberalism is completely wrapped up with the notion of self. The legacy of the sixties' "if it feels good do it" ethos is alive and well. Modern liberals, as we shall see, often embrace these teachings and incorporate them in the way they live their lives and maintain their relationships.

For dramatic proof, go to the streets of a liberal enclave like San Francisco, Seattle, or Vermont. There will be plenty of expensive boutiques, antique dealers, health spas, sushi bars, and upscale coffee shops. But you won't see very many children. The reason is not that right-wingers have dumped buckets of birth control pills into the San Francisco municipal water supply. The simple fact is that many on the liberal-left today just don't want to have children.

A 2004 survey showed that a typical sample of 100 unrelated adults who called themselves liberal will have 147 children. That contrasts with the typical conservative, who is likely to have 208 children per 100 unrelated adults. That's 41 percent more.[3] Why is this important? Because raising children is a difficult and selfless act that is also an important civic duty. The survival of our society—not to mention our Social Security system!—rests on individuals bringing up a new generation.

The liberal Northeastern states—Vermont, Maine, Massachusetts, and New York—have the lowest fertility rates in the country. They also have the lowest percentage of population under the age of five. In progressive San Francisco, there are more dogs than children. Joel Kotkin points out that Seattle (my hometown) has roughly the same population as it did in the 1960s, but barely half as many children. Indeed, there are nearly 45 percent more dogs than children.[4] Dogs, of course, offer companionship without the burdens and responsibilities of children.

Some might conclude that this is a result of the high cost of living in desirable cities like Boston, New York, and San Francisco. But in these childless meccas we also see some of the highest per capita expenditures on luxury goods, spas, and personal therapies. (Kotkin regards San Francisco as a "childless liberal boutique city.")[5] It's not a lack of money; it's a lack of interest. The General Social Survey found that 69 percent of those who called themselves "very conservative" said it was important to them to have children. Only 38 percent of corresponding liberals agreed. An online survey (admittedly not scientific) taken by the left-wing website daily kos.com asked readers if they had children and how many. The most popular answers: "No children," "Not going to have any," and "Don't want any."

Meanwhile, the highest fertility rate in the country is found in the most conservative state, Utah, followed by Arizona, Alaska, and Texas, otherwise known as "red states," according to the latest National Center for Health Statistics survey. States with the lowest fertility rates are Maine, Massachusetts, and Rhode Island, all "blue states." Over half of the women of childbearing age—15 to 44—are childless in liberal bastions such as the District of Columbia, Vermont, and Massachusetts.[6]

Many on the left proudly proclaim themselves to be "child-free." (They angrily reject the term child-*less* because it implies that they are missing out on something.) Partly this is a result of liberal pessimism about the future. Concerned about overpopulation, dwindling environmental resources, global warming, etc., some liberals don't want to have children because they see them as an environmental hazard. Billionaire Ted Turner reflected this attitude when he thoughtfully announced his regret at having five children. "If I was doing it over again, I wouldn't have had that many, but I can't shoot them now and they're here."[7] No doubt this sort of sentiment makes for charming conversation around the Turner dinner table.

Far more common is the modern liberal notion that children are a burden, something that will get in the way of one's self-fulfillment. As any parent knows, raising children is hard work. It requires emotional commitment, selfless acts, large quantities of time, and scads of money. Many liberals just don't want the inconvenience. When asked by the World Values Survey whether parents should sacrifice their own well-being for those of their children, those on the left were nearly twice as likely to say "no" (28 percent to 15 percent) when compared to conservatives.[8]

A look at some popular websites offers plenty of evidence that this is a major strand in modern liberal thinking: "The trouble is, many of us bright, liberal people know that procreation is a quaint, antiquated concept." And another: "I read somewhere a while back that it costs about 1 Million to raise a child from birth to 21 years assuming they attend college. So buy a house in SF or have a kid? I'm not actually looking for an answer but kids are expensive." And another: "I'll have the babies if you pay for them."[9]

Another offers: "I have not been asked very often why I'm childless. If I am I just say the truth. That I am too selfish, that I want to spend my time and money on things other than children, that I am doing my part to counteract all of the over-breeders. The thought of attending a child's athletic event, and sitting through the whole thing, is almost enough in itself."[10] Peter Pan could not have put it better.

This birth gap presents a quandary for politically active liberals. Not wanting to be inconvenienced with raising their own children, they still want to see their ideas perpetuated. Professor Darren Sherkat of Southern Illinois University worries that because conservatives "who have lots of children" are not being matched by those on the political left who "may well not have kids," these demographic trends will push the country in a more conservative direction. (Data indicates that 80 percent of children end up adopting the political attitudes of their parents.) To counterbalance this trend, he argues for increasing immigration and expanding the black population. He also hopes that childless liberals will "be able to reproduce themselves in strangers," by taking on jobs as teachers, writers, and other people of influence. The idea is to let conservatives raise their children, while liberals influence them through the schools and universities.[11] One liberal proposes a more extreme solution: "We could just start kidnapping those babies of conservative parents and raise them to be ACLU-card toting liberals. That would address the imbalance without raising populations."[12] The last comment is a joke, of course, but it highlights a disturbing reality: Liberals who express little interest in having children of their own want control over how other peoples' children are raised.

As Hillary Clinton once told *Newsweek*, "There is no such thing as other people's children."

Another lefty concurs: "I'd say that the author of a popular book has far more aggregate influence than do one set of parents. So if the book is very popular and captures the imaginations of kids, presto, you've done a lot to insure that the ideas that are important to you live long after you pass on. . . . If it's the ideas that matter then I suppose that there are ways that folks like you can propagate the ideas without having your own kids be your lab rats."[13]

This lack of interest in raising children is matched by the lack of enthusiasm among liberals for making a commitment to marriage. Many on the left prefer to fly solo because marriage gets in the way of their individual freedom. According to the General Social Survey, 65 percent of those who were very conservative said marriage was important to them, compared with just 30 percent who were very liberal. Nearly half on the left (48 percent) said it was "not at all important."[14]

This should not be surprising to anyone paying attention to the drift of liberal thinking over the past forty years. While a majority of liberals clearly still prefer the security and rewards of married life—although they may go through several spouses in their restless search for the ideal partner—many on the "progressive" left have a clear disdain for family life.[15] Barbara Ehrenreich, a popular fixture on college campuses and a bestselling lefty author and columnist, has written: "There is a long and honorable tradition of 'anti-family' thought." She approvingly quotes Charles Fourier, the French philosopher who "taught that the family was a barrier to human progress," and British anthropologist Edmund Leach, who said, "Far from being the basis of a good society, the family with its narrow privacy and tawdry secrets is the source of all discontents." In another *Time* essay, the twice-married Ehrenreich slammed marriage and encouraged transitory and ad hoc relationships. She hoped that in the future, kids would be raised by communal groups of adults.[16]

Meanwhile, law professor Catharine MacKinnon declares that "feminism stresses the indistinguishability of prostitution, marriage, and sexual harassment." Feminist Vivian Gornick has claimed that "being a housewife is an illegitimate profession."[17]

Professor Linda Hirshman of Brandeis says that "the Family—with its repetitious, socially invisible, physical tasks—is a necessary part of life, but it allows fewer opportunities for full human flourishing than public spheres like the market or the government."[18] That's no doubt how Peter Pan would view it, absent the academic language.

Nobel laureate Toni Morrison likewise observed, "The little nuclear family is a paradigm that just doesn't work. . . . Why we are hanging on to it, I don't know." The National Organization for Women has over the years distributed a bumper sticker that proclaims: "One Nuclear Family Can Ruin Your Whole Life." Alice Rossi, former head of the American Sociological Association, explains that a broad alliance on the left now shares the view that "the nuclear family and monogamous marriage are oppressive, sexist, 'bourgeois,' and sick."[19]

Gloria Steinem advised two generations of young people to seek out self-love rather than loving someone else. "The truth is finding ourselves brings more excitement and well-being than anything romance can offer," she wrote in her 1992 book *Revolution from Within.*[20]

Adrianne Frost, a self-described feminist comedian and onetime correspondent for Comedy Central's *The Daily Show,* has written a book called *I Hate Other People's Kids.*

The more highbrow *Washington Monthly* has featured such articles as "The Case Against Kids," which explains how parents should not sacrifice their careers for their children.[21]

Other feminists complain about the inconveniences posed by parents with children. One childless feminist professes to be put out because "everyone will make way for a woman with a stroller or a child in tow."[22] Professor Debra Mollen at Texas Woman's University complains that "pregnant women get preferential parking."[23]

Professor Christopher Clausen, writing in *American Scholar,* notes that "in intellectual circles the phrase 'family values' has become a term of ridicule," in part because so few liberal academics are interested in the burdens of having children. He points out the attraction that going childless—excuse me, child-free—poses for academics on the left. This interest has less to do with high-minded idealism than with preventing children from distracting you from yourself. He notes that he admires a friend of the family who decided not to have children, in contrast to his own parents. "They liked their freedom too much. Although the man was subordinate to my father at the National Institutes of Health, the couple inhabited a cavernous eighteenth-century house in Georgetown instead of, like us, a suburban three-bedroom in Bethesda. They had no need to worry about local schools and playgrounds. They took trips to New York whenever they wanted, and occasionally to Europe. They frequently ate in restaurants."[24] All the important things in life.

Linda Hirshman gets down to brass tacks in her book *Get*

to Work: A Manifesto for Women of the World, a clarion call for women to be more self-focused. Why avoid having children? Because they get in the way of reaching your full potential, Hirshman explains. The only life worth living is one that includes a high income and a satisfying career. Having kids and staying home to kiss boo-boos is a losing proposition. She advises women to "find the money."[25]

When Rabbi Shmuley Boteach published an essay on the Internet about the contempt that many liberals show toward parents of large families, he was barraged with nasty e-mails upbraiding him for the idea that large families are good. Some of them called people with large families "breeders." One wrote: "What is the income tax deduction for 10 children? It comes to $32,000 doesn't it? Now, if that religious person happens to give, for example, $5,000 tithing to his church, the first thing you know they are paying little or no taxes while the rest of us are paying through the nose."[26]

A friend of a friend reports that on a recent trip to Cambridge, Massachusetts, pushing a stroller with several other children in tow, she was actually spit at by a local resident concerned about overpopulating the planet. Of course, when the childless man grows old, he will no doubt be living off the taxes provided by this lady's children.[27]

This will no doubt come as a surprise to those who are used to hearing leftists talk about the need to help America's children. Modern liberals profess a love for children—supporting an array of social programs designed to help them. In his book *Conscience of a Liberal,* the late senator Paul Wellstone (D-MN) wrote a chapter on helping children. But the chapter was entirely about government programs and spending federal tax dollars. These programs are seen as the true test of one's commitment to children. When Republicans talked of cutting back on social spending, Bill Clinton declared that they wanted to "make war on the kids in this country." Congressman Major Owens accused them of "practicing genocide with a smile." Mario Cuomo, during the 1984 Democratic Convention, painted conservatives as uncaring toward the young and the elderly. "The Republicans believe the wagon train will not make it to the frontier unless some of our old, some of our young, and some of our weak are left behind by the side of the trail. We Democrats believe that we can make it all the way with the whole family intact."[28]

Supporting government programs to "help the children" is a convenient way for liberals to "love" children without demanding anything of themselves. Supporting government programs that allegedly help children is the perfect path to commitment-free living. Responsibility is limited to paying one's taxes. All this amounts to what Kay Hymowitz of the Manhattan Institute calls "postmodern postadolescence," an approach to life glamorized in the television show *Seinfeld*: avoid encumbrances, commitments, and responsibilities, and guard your independence and autonomy at all costs.

Modern liberalism seems to promote narcissism. Professors at Smith College and George Washington University discovered this when they conducted a study of 1,195 college students at four American universities (Harvard, Michigan,

Massachusetts, and Boston). What they discovered was that those who were very liberal or radical tended to have a "narcissistic pathology," which included "grandiosity, envy, a lack of empathy, illusion of personal perfection, and a sense of entitlement." These self-described liberals and leftists were very self-absorbed and self-confident in a way that reflected an "egocentrism exceeding what we normally think of as healthy self-esteem." They also found that liberals were "the most power oriented" of the students surveyed. Similar results were found when the same study was conducted in Germany.[29]

Partly this results from the fact that conservatives are more likely to believe they are accountable to something greater than themselves, namely God. Three professors at the University of Tennessee gave an extensive survey to more than three hundred college students. They discovered that conservative religious students were much less likely to be self-absorbed and narcissistic than others.[30] Perhaps then there should be little surprise that when the World Values Survey asked Americans "How do you maintain good relations with people—by understanding others' preferences or by expressing your own?" 49 percent of left-wing respondents said expressing your own preferences was the most important. Only 28 percent on the right agreed.[31]

What about helping a friend in need? A survey of more than two thousand American adults found that when the question was asked—Should you always help a friend in need?—95 percent of those who were conservative said yes, compared with only 79 percent of self-described progressives.[32] Not coincidentally, perhaps, conservatives also tend to get more satisfaction out of their close personal relationships. When asked how much satisfaction they got out of their friendships, conservatives were more likely to say a very great deal, and a great deal more than liberals. When it came to getting satisfaction out of their family life, 53 percent of those who considered themselves very conservative said a "very great deal," compared with 40 percent who said they were very liberal.[33]

Nor is it surprising to find that liberals are more alienated and detached from their families. Research by Professor Randy Thornhill and Corey Fincher found that conservatives are much more likely to report secure childhoods and strong attachments to one or both parents. Liberals on the other hand reported higher levels of stress and dissatisfaction with their family lives.[34] The World Values Survey found that conservatives were much more likely to report feeling very close to their mother and father than liberals. And liberals were much less likely to say that their own parents were close: only 36 percent, compared with 66 percent of conservatives. Nor do liberals trust members of their family as much as conservatives. Fully 94 percent of conservatives said they had a lot of trust in other members of their family, compared with only 69 percent of liberals. (It is interesting to note that many leading feminists, including Gloria Steinem and Betty Friedan, had difficulty with their families as they were growing up.)

In addition, many progressives view personal commitments to friends and relatives as something that can be broken if they prove too "inconvenient." More than half (51 percent) of progressives said it was okay to break a promise to family or friends if it proved "too difficult or inconvenient," compared with only 31 percent of conservatives.[35]

Liberals are correspondingly less likely to rely on their families for help and advice than conservatives. For one thing, they don't talk to their parents nearly as much. More than half (58 percent) of conservatives said they had been in touch with dad by telephone or letter in the past week, compared with only 30 percent of corresponding liberals. Moms don't do much better. Almost three-quarters of conservatives talked to their mothers once a week by phone, compared with just over half of liberals.

Who do liberals say they will turn to if they face a problem in life? They are most likely to avoid talking to their parents and instead rely on the advice of friends. Having a marital problem? The most popular choice for those on the left is a friend (39 percent). Far down the list were their spouse (4 percent) or their mother (13 percent). In contrast, for those who described themselves as very conservative, a family member or spouse was the more likely choice. Short of cash? Liberals again tend to look to their "closest friend" for money. (Those with liberal friends—watch your wallets.) Meanwhile, those who were very conservative mentioned family members as their first choice.

Liberals are also twice as likely to say that they "make an effort to live up to what my friends expect." There's nothing wrong with valuing your friends' opinions, of course, as long as you do it for the right reasons. For many liberals, that reason appears to be nothing more profound than popularity. When asked what is most important to prepare a child for life, 40 percent of liberals listed "being popular" among them— compared with only 24 percent of conservatives. On the other hand, conservatives were more likely to say one of their main goals in life was to "make my parents proud."[36]

Even when liberals do have children they tend to outsource their parental responsibilities. Hillary Clinton has pushed the notion that "it takes a village" to raise a child. But the village she has in mind is the federal government, and many on the left take that to mean that the federal government will fulfill their parenting responsibilities. This is not to suggest that liberals cannot be good parents. But professors at Princeton and Mississippi State found that conservatives "are significantly more likely than other parents to display positive, nurturing emotions toward their children." Many liberals seem to think that conservatism is a form of mental illness, a crabbed and selfish outlook bred in childhood by abusive and withholding parents. But while the study found that conservatives were "more inclined to spank their children," they are "also more likely to express love and affection toward them." Conservatives were markedly less likely to yell at their children, and more likely to hug them. (Perhaps their liberal counterparts were too busy hugging trees.)[37]

Another study using data from the National Survey of Families and Households found: "Conservative fathers are more likely to be involved with their children in personal activities such as personal talks" than those who were not conservative.[38] Moreover—contradicting the liberal stereotype of conservatives as prudish and uptight—conservatives are more likely to talk with their children about sex than those who are liberal or don't attend church. Indeed, according to a researcher at the University of Texas, 47 percent of parents who attended church weekly (and the vast majority of these are conservatives) talked with their children "a great deal" about sex. Only 32 percent of parents who don't attend church talk to their kids about sex.

This doesn't mean that liberals fail to pass their permissive sexual attitudes on to their offspring. Quite the contrary. As a researcher at the University of Wisconsin found: "The more liberal teens think their mothers' sexual opinions are, the more likely they are to have had sex and the more sexual partners they are likely to have."[39] One study from the *Journal of Adolescent Health* found that the daughters of conservatives have less premarital sex than the children of liberals.[40]

The liberal push for unrestricted "freedom" plays a role here, too. When asked how important it is for "men to have more freedom" in child rearing so they can "do other things," liberal men were much more likely to say such freedom is of paramount importance (50 percent of liberals, compared with 40 percent of conservatives).[41]

Some liberals are openly disdainful of what they consider "old-fashioned" parenting methods. "My father and I had so little common ground that we had almost no basis for emotional connection," recalls TV producer Don Reo. "That isn't true now. We children of the 60s who now have children of our own are far less 'parental.' We can relate—because we have rock n' roll in common." David Denby of the *New Yorker* likewise defends this fashionable hands-off approach: He and his wife refuse "to stand over the children, guiding their progress all day long like missionaries leading savages to light. To assume control over their habits and attitudes, we would have to become bullies."[42]

It seems that many on the left are looking to "the village" to do what they are supposed to do as parents.

The tendency for liberals to focus on themselves extends to the way they look at life as a quest for personal meaning and fulfillment. In a now-famous speech at the University of Texas in 1993, Hillary Clinton wondered out loud about "the crisis of meaning" that she perceived was ailing our society: "What do our governmental institutions mean? What do our lives in today's world mean? . . . What do all of our institutions mean? What does it mean to be educated? What does it mean to be a journalist? What does it mean in today's world to pursue not only vocations, to be part of institutions, but to be human?" In the face of this vacuum of meaning that she and other liberals experience, she called for a "new politics of meaning" that would answer life's great questions and make us all good citizens, spouses, and parents.

Most conservatives, however, have no need of a new redemptive vision of politics to fill their lives with meaning. Many find the sense of meaning Hillary seems to lack in their religious faith or by adhering to a moral code that is outside of and superior to themselves. In contrast, liberalism has turned its adherents away from the search for larger truths and exhorts them to find the meaning of life within themselves.

When the General Social Survey asked whether "life has meaning only if you provide meaning," an interesting pattern emerged. The farther left you go, the more likely people are to agree with that sentiment. Modern liberals also don't like the idea of good and evil and would rather create their own notions of what is good and bad. Only 23 percent of those who call themselves "very liberal" say that there are objective guidelines about what is good and evil, compared with 62 percent of conservatives. Many liberals also don't like the idea that they need to pay attention to someone or something greater than themselves. Only 40 percent consider God very important in their lives, compared with 70 percent of conservatives.[43]

For those who want something "spiritual" in their lives without demanding very much, the New Age movement is the logical home. The New Age mantra that "all spiritual truth is within me" appeals to the Mighty Me. New Age teachers talk about self-awareness, self-realization, self-knowledge, and finding truth within yourself. In the sixties the motto was "find yourself." New Agers have embraced this self-absorbed notion and turned it into big business.

Academic studies confirm that those who buy New Age books, tapes, and DVDs are overwhelmingly liberal in their politics. As Wendy Kaminer (a critic of both religion and spirituality in general) has noted, the New Age movement is particularly self-absorbed. It is the perfect religion for Peter Pan: All the deep spiritual answers are to be found within ourselves—and there are none of the inconvenient demands of conventional religions.[44]

One of the most selfish and narcissistic habits in modern America is drug abuse. Here again we find the fingerprints of liberalism. The liberal search for autonomy and the credo "if it feels good do it" have a strong influence on who uses drugs and why. Many liberals denounce drug use as a danger while at the same time engaging in a wink-wink attitude toward its actual use. When President Bill Clinton was famously asked by a student on MTV in 1992 about his implausible statement that he had tried marijuana but never inhaled, he had an opportunity to address the question of drug use seriously. Instead, he turned it into a joke and said that if he could do it over again, he probably *would* have inhaled. The Clinton White House was notable for its tolerant attitude toward drugs. When Clinton spokesman Mike McCurry was asked about his own past history of drug use during a press conference, he responded: "You know, did I smoke a joint from time to time? Of course I did." As if to say, who wouldn't?[45]

Recreational drug use by responsible adults may be one legacy of the sixties that we simply have to live with, and many conservatives—especially libertarians—are willing to condone it. But no one can behold the ravages of teenage drug abuse and heavy narcotic addiction and not be appalled at their toll. Nor can it be denied that elite attitudes play a role in shaping broader public opinion and behavior. As we have seen in the case of smoking and drunk driving, public opprobrium can be a powerful force. Yet liberal elites promote an indulgent attitude toward drugs that does real harm to impressionable youngsters.

Bonnie Erbe, a PBS talk show host and lefty columnist who relishes bashing conservatives, bragged about what she had accomplished while taking drugs. "Prior to trying heroin I smoked a lot of different types of marijuana and hashish (yes, inhaling all the time) and took a wide variety of hallucinogens: mescaline, LSD, you name it. Well, I not only survived that stupor, I excelled at high school studies and extracurricular activities during it."[46]

CNN reporter Stephanie Elam did a story about legalizing drugs and referred humorously to "our friend marijuana."[47] When comedian Al Franken was asked about the use of drugs on the set of *Saturday Night Live,* he explained: "I only did cocaine to stay awake and make sure nobody else did too much cocaine. That was the only reason I did it. Hehheh."[48] HBO television personality Bill Maher has actively pushed for the legalization of marijuana and said that he is "willing to do his part. . . . I will be a martyr for this cause."

Modern liberalism's celebration of the drug culture was in full force when Hunter S. Thompson died in 2005. Thompson, author of *Fear and Loathing in Las Vegas,* among other works, was widely considered the "living bible of the drug culture" by his fans. Thompson embraced the drug culture. "I hate to advocate drugs, alcohol, violence, or insanity to anyone," he famously said, "but they've always worked for me." On another occasion he explained how using drugs made him a better writer. Thompson's funeral (caused by suicide) brought out Sen. John Kerry, George McGovern, CBS News heavyweight Ed Bradley, and Hollywood liberals Johnny Depp and Sean Penn to pay homage. "I wouldn't miss this for the world," Kerry told a reporter as he boarded a plane with his arm around McGovern. "I met Hunter in the days of Vietnam Veterans Against the War. Then, last summer, I offered him the vice presidency in jest. He's missed."[49]

Thompson's example was not lost on young people around the country. According to Thompson's widow, her husband's death brought forth "stacks of e-mails and letters from young people" who were eager to find success through drugs. "They wrote me these letters about drinking bottles of Wild Turkey and doing grams of cocaine," she said.[50]

Actor Johnny Depp forked over $2 million to erect a giant tower for the funeral. The structure, larger than the Statue of Liberty, was used to shoot Thompson's ashes into the sky, something he had requested before his death. The *New York Times* described it as "a rocket-like structure embedded with a dagger. It was crowned by Mr. Thompson's logo, a two-and-a-half-ton red fist with two thumbs and a psychedelic peyote button pulsating at its center."[51]

There has been similar lionization of Abbie Hoffman, the

former sixties radical who personified the liberal-left attitude for much of his life. He was the subject of an adoring film, *Steal This Movie,* starring Vincent D'Onofrio and Janeane Garofalo. The movie poster features a shot of Hoffman smoking a joint. When he died of a suicidal overdose of drugs and alcohol, he was proclaimed a "hero of the sixties" by the *San Jose Mercury News,* and columnist Ellen Goodman praised him for "living sixties values in an eighties world." (Note: This is high praise.) Hoffman died, she says, with his "integrity intact." The *New York Times* gave him an obituary titled "Peace and Environmental Activist Dies." All this in spite of the fact that Hoffman was immersed in the drug culture. He was convicted of selling cocaine and avoided police capture for years. He dismissed selling cocaine to young people as no big deal. "[Drug] dealing," he once said, "although dangerous, is a tax-free way of surviving, even though it borders on work."[52]

Abe Rosenthal, former executive editor of the *New York Times,* once pointed out that liberal intellectuals are out of touch when it comes to fighting drug abuse, and seem unable to recognize that there is such a thing as taking tolerance too far. President Reagan came to the same conclusion, accusing a permissive "liberal elite" of undercutting his war on drugs.[53] But the sixties' left believed that some drugs were better than others. Tom Coffin explained it in the alternative newspaper *Great Speckled Bird*: "Dope not Drugs—alcohol is a drug, pot is DOPE; nicotine is a drug, acid is DOPE; drugs turn you off, dull your senses, give you the strength to face another day in Death America; DOPE turns you on, heightens sensory awareness, sometimes twists them out of shape and you experience that too, gives you vision and clarity, necessary to create Life From Death."

Few would be so bold as to say this publicly today—and the vast majority on the left have pulled away from directly endorsing drug use. (That would garner too much criticism.) But there is little question that while the left appears intensely interested in curtailing tobacco consumption, it actively promotes legalization of marijuana. During the Clinton administration, for example, the Office of National Drug Control Policy was slashed from 147 full-time positions to 25. The Customs Service cut 662 jobs, meaning thousands of fewer drug import convictions. And while Clinton administration officials aggressively pushed to reduce teen smoking, they suppressed the sale of home drug-testing kits for parents on the grounds that they might create family tension.[54]

That attitude seems to have trickled down to rank-and-file liberals. Modern liberals are much more likely to use drugs than conservatives. Academic studies have found that those on the political left are five times more likely to use marijuana and cocaine. Another study (that compared people by political identification) found the same result. A third found "a direct and linear relationship between political leftism and the use of any single illicit drug."[55]

Those proclivities also influence which kids end up using drugs. Researchers at the University of Southern California and UCLA found that "liberalism" was a determining factor in whether children use drugs. They found that "acceptance of traditional values" actually leads to lower drug use by children. Children whose parents were not liberal translated into "less drug problems and fewer property crimes."[56] Does this mean that all the children of liberals will use drugs and those of conservatives won't? Of course not. But the data is clear: Liberalism promotes or condones drug use among those who embrace its ideas.[57]

If liberals really want to stamp out teen smoking, perhaps they should encourage more young people to be conservatives. One survey of high school students found that among seniors, liberals were more than twice as likely to get drunk and smoke as conservatives. Another study found that liberalism was strongly "associated with cigarette use and cocaine use."[58]

Given the liberal ethic of autonomy and hedonism, it should come as no surprise that when it comes to using illicit drugs, liberals have a significant leg up. Surveys have shown that liberals are five times more likely than conservatives to have used marijuana and cocaine.[59] Another survey found that Democrats were five times more likely to use marijuana than Republicans. (Those administering the survey said the results were somewhat incomplete. Several of the surveys were rejected "because the respondent indicated that he had been intoxicated with marijuana while he was filling out the questionnaire.")[60] Finally, a study published in the *American Journal of Drug and Alcohol Abuse* found that among heavy drug users, the ratio of Democrats to Republicans was more than 8 to 1.[61]

Could this gap be a result of liberals being more honest when asked these questions? The answer is a resounding no. Research shows that conservatives are just as likely to answer drug-related questions honestly.[62]

In the past, says Robert Bork, "Men were kept from rootless hedonism, which is the end stage of unconfined individualism, by religion, morality, and law." Without these restraints, man will pursue selfishness with greater zeal. That is the fate of modern liberalism. Whether or not liberalism causes these effects, it certainly provides a handy justification for a lot of self-centered and self-indulgent behavior. Modern liberalism, as a philosophy and way of life, provides the best means to pursue the interests of the Mighty Me. As a liberal in good standing, you can outsource your responsibilities and focus on what's really important—yourself—with nary a twinge of conscience.

2.

THINK GLOBALLY, SIT ON YOUR BUTT LOCALLY Or, Why Conservatives Are Actually More Generous Than Liberals

Samuel Johnson once reported on a man who was privately stingy but publicly touted the merits of sharing and philanthropy. Dr. Johnson said sarcastically that the man was a "friend of goodness." What he meant was that flesh-and-blood goodness is very different from supporting Goodness in the abstract.[1]

One of the most common conceits of modern liberalism is that those on the left are selfless and altruistic while conservatives are selfish and stingy. The main reason people have this impression is that liberals and leftists regularly brag about how generous they are. This, for example, is how the *New York Times* described the courtship of Kerry Kennedy (of guess which family) and Andrew Cuomo, now attorney general of New York: "Ms. Kennedy-Cuomo, 43, said she fell in love with Mr. Cuomo, 45, when he took her on a tour of a homeless shelter on their first date and agreed to fast for the labor leader Cesar Chavez."[2]

Political liberals often boast about these moments of sensitivity, such as the first time they saw a child in poverty and committed their lives to fighting injustice. Sometimes the epiphany doesn't even have to involve other people. In her autobiography, Hillary Clinton recalled her first semester at Wellesley. There had been a heavy snowfall and a fellow student came running up to her in a panic. Together they went out into the cold and began shaking the snow off of tree limbs in order to save them. "It was then I knew that was where I belonged," she explained.[3]

Liberals today are completely convinced that they are noble, sensitive, and concerned about others while conservatives are selfish and greedy. "I am a liberal," says Garrison Keillor of *Prairie Home Companion* fame, "and liberalism is the politics of kindness." Republicans, says the mayor of Lake Wobegon, don't care about the suffering around them. "To the hard-assed redneck Republican tax cutter of the suburbs, human misery is all a fiction, something out of novels, stories of matchstick people." Kids who get physically abused? Conservatives consider them "roadkill." The Republican ideology is a "screw you philosophy," writes Keillor, offering "the guarantee of the right to be a jerk." Liberals on the other hand "don't let people lie in the ditch and drive past and pretend not to see them dying."[4] (Apparently this has been going on for some time in red-state America.)

This rarely challenged claim of liberal philanthropy and conservative stinginess has become a standard staple of political campaigns. Hillary Clinton says that conservatives appeal to the "mighty me." Jimmy Carter says "selfishness rules" in conservative thinking. Conservative students hear this all the time. One Harvard student wrote in the student newspaper of being told by a friend, "You can't be a conservative Republican; you're not heartless!"[5]

When Professor Arthur Brooks of Syracuse University released his heavily researched book *Who Really Cares?*— which demonstrated that conservatives gave more to charity than liberals—it was completely ignored by the media. The *New York Times* and *Washington Post* never reviewed the book or published an article about it (although the *Times* did run an op-ed piece criticizing it). Likewise, CNN and NPR devoted no airtime to Brooks's findings.[6]

But the reality is that liberals are often, like Dr. Johnson's acquaintance, "friends of goodness," loudly proclaiming their commitment to social justice while in practice being stingy and frequently unwilling to help those less fortunate. Conservatives, in contrast, tend to be more giving and helpful in practice.

Consider the case of Andrew Cuomo, who apparently takes dates to homeless shelters to demonstrate his sensitivity and social concern. The current attorney general of New York, Cuomo is the former head of a commission on the homeless in New York City, and explains on his website that he has "compassion toward the most vulnerable of us."[7] But *advocating* for the homeless and occasionally visiting them in a shelter should not be confused with actually *giving* to the homeless. Cuomo was a housing advocate throughout the 1990s, but according to his publicly available tax returns, he made *no* charitable contributions between 1996 and 1999. In 2000 he donated a whopping $2,750. In 2004 and 2005, Cuomo had more than $1.5 million in adjusted gross income but gave a paltry $2,000 to charity. He made no charitable contributions in 2003, when his income was a bit less than $300,000.[8]

Cuomo is not alone in his hypocrisy. In December 1998, Vice President Al Gore gave a speech to the Democratic Leadership Council on the importance of helping others. "Compassion is more than a pretty word: It is the highest of all disciplines," he assured the audience of thousands.[9] Unfortunately, Gore had not mastered the discipline himself. His tax returns for that year reveal that Gore gave just $353 to charity, out of an adjusted gross income of $197,729. (That same year, other Americans reporting an income of $100,000 to $200,000 gave an average of $3,377 to charity.)[10]

Initially, Gore's defense was that they had donated more than that, often in the form of "food and clothing to the homeless." But when no one could provide evidence that homeless people were wearing Gore's cast-off suits or Tipper's gowns, the defense quickly changed. Gore spokesman Chris Lehane offered the typical "friend of goodness" response, explaining that "to truly judge a person's commitment to helping others, you need to consider what they have done with their lives and how they have spent their time—and by that standard the Gores are extraordinarily committed." Had Gore been putting in time at a homeless shelter or soup kitchen? Of course not. Lehane was talking about the fact that Gore was committed to "public service," or politics, which apparently is considered by some to be charitable work.[11]

Gore's speech about compassion reflected the thinking that has become all too common among those on the political left. Gore didn't talk so much about individuals being compassionate. He talked about being compassionate with other people's money. "Compassion means reserving the surplus until we save Social Security first, so that all Americans have the retirement they deserve," Gore said. He never advocated volunteering or donating to charity. Compassion apparently begins and ends with government programs.[12]

Vice President Gore might have been off by a factor of ten when it came to making charitable contributions compared to average Americans, but he's downright benevolent when compared to Sen. John Kerry. In 1995, Kerry reported a taxable income of $126,179—but gave nothing to charity. That same year, according to records, he spent $500,000 to buy a half stake in a seventeenth-century Dutch seascape painting by Adam Willaerts. In 1994, Kerry did muster $2,039 in charitable contributions, still well below the national average. In 1993, he gave $175 to the needy. That same year he managed to scrape together $8,000 to buy a Ducati Italian motorcycle. Later, Kerry married millionairess Theresa Heinz, and today he is active in charitable causes, using the Heinz Foundation as his vehicle.[13]

Fellow Massachusetts senator Edward Kennedy has clearly relished his role over the years as a liberal Robin Hood, taking from the rich and giving to the poor. His speeches are generously sprinkled with statements about heartless Republicans and compassionate liberals. Typical of such Robin Hood statements is this one he made to Al Hunt of the *Wall Street Journal*: "I come from an advantaged life, and I'll be goddamned if I'm going to get re-elected to the U.S. Senate by taking food out of the mouths of needy children." While these sorts of statements are common, they should not be confused with Senator Kennedy actually *giving* much money to needy children.[14]

Ted Kennedy's tax returns are obviously a closely guarded secret. But when he chose to run for president in the 1970s, he released some of them. What they reveal is that Kennedy gave very little to charity. With a net worth of more than $8 million in the early 1970s and an annual income of $461,444 from a series of family trusts, Senator Robin Hood gave barely 1 percent of his income to charity. The sum is about as much as Kennedy claimed as a write-off on his fifty-foot sailing sloop *Curragh*.[15]

Robert Reich, once Bill Clinton's secretary of labor and

now a professor at UC-Berkeley, has been an outspoken liberal writer and speaker throughout his career. He has written several bestsellers, all of which explain how greedy and uncaring conservatives are. Conservatives believe in "reviving social Darwinism," and because of conservatives, "America has placed too high a value on selfishness," says Reich.[16]

When he ran for governor of Massachusetts in 2002, Reich was all but forced to release his tax returns in the Democratic primary. It's not a pretty picture. (He filed jointly with his wife, Clare Dalton, a Northeastern University law professor.) Reich's 1040 revealed an income of more than $1 million, much of it from giving speeches to corporations and universities for up to $40,000 a pop. During those lectures he explained the need for the haves to give more to the have-nots and denounced the prevalence of "greed" in America.

But according to Reich's own tax returns, he contributed just $2,714 of his million-dollar income to charity that year. (For those keeping track, that amounts to 0.2 percent.) And not all of that was cash. Seven hundred dollars was claimed for donating his son's old drum set to an organization called City of Peace. Reich's explanation for this lack of charity? He was too busy to make charitable contributions at the time.[17]

During the 2006 election, the darling of the liberal-left was Democratic Senate nominee Ned Lamont, a multimillionaire whom many regarded as a savior in the struggle to defeat Sen. Joe Lieberman, who was deemed too conservative because of his support for the War on Terror. Lefty websites like Daily Kos embraced Lamont as a genuine man of the left.

It helped, of course, that Lamont was worth more than $200 million, much of it inherited. According to Lamont's tax return, he made $2.8 million in 2005 and donated $5,385 in charitable contributions (.027 percent of his income to be exact). That same year he bought a $1 million piece of art. During the campaign, Lamont talked about the need to raise taxes because the wealthy were not doing enough to help those in need.[18]

The greatest liberal icon of the twentieth century is Franklin Delano Roosevelt. Regarded by many on the left as the personification of charity and compassion, Roosevelt and his wife spoke often of the need for those with wealth to share their money with those less fortunate. During the 1936 Democratic Party Convention, for example, he defined charity as one of the great virtues. "For charity literally translated from the original means love, the love that understands, that does not merely share the wealth of the giver, but in true sympathy and wisdom helps men to help themselves." He also spoke in favor of a government with a "spirit of charity." He challenged political opponents for their greed and "heedless self-interest." He reminded everyone that "charity begins at home."

But Roosevelt's compassion seemed only to extend to other people's money. There might have been an economic depression in which one-third of the country was "ill-housed, ill-clad, and ill-nourished." Yet according to his tax returns, in his most charitable year Roosevelt made more than $93,000 (more than $1.3 million today), but gave away about 3 percent of his income to charity during the height of the Great Depression. At this time Roosevelt was a very wealthy man, with extensive holdings in real estate and the stock market. In other years, 1935 for example, he gave away just 2 percent of his income.

This evidence of liberal hypocrisy is damning enough. But what really amazes is how poorly these liberals do in comparison to so-called "heartless conservatives." President Ronald Reagan was often criticized for being callous toward the less fortunate and ushering in a gilded age of materialism. He advanced an ethos of "greed"—or so said critics like Katie Couric. Unlike Roosevelt or JFK, Reagan was not a wealthy man when he became president. He had no family trust or investment portfolio to fall back on. And yet according to his tax returns, he donated more than *four times* more to charity—both in terms of actual money and on a percentage basis—than Sen. Ted Kennedy. And he gave more to charities with less income than FDR did during the height of the Depression. In 1985, for example, he gave away 6 percent of his income to charity.[19]

President George W. Bush and Vice President Dick Cheney have also proven to be more charitable than their liberal critics. Back in 1991, when Bush was a private citizen, he had a reported income of $179,591 and donated an enormous $28,236 to charity. (That same year Bill and Hillary Clinton made almost twice as much but contributed the same amount.) In 1992, Bush reported income of $212,313 and contributions of $31,914. In 1993, Bush reported income of $610,772, and contributions of $31,292. Clearly there is something to Bush's belief in the power of faith-based charities.

While president, Bush's charitable giving has increased. In 2005 he gave away more than 10 percent of his income. In contrast, former senator John Edwards, who often bemoans the "two Americas" of rich and poor, and is a wealthier man than Bush, gave less. Sen. Barack Obama, who likewise talks regularly about his concern and compassion for the less fortunate, gives far less to charity than Bush. In 2005 he made $1.7 million (more than 2.5 times what President Bush made) but gave the same dollar amount as Bush. In 2006, Bush made a third less than Obama, but actually gave more to charity.[20]

When Vice President Dick Cheney decided to donate 77 percent of his income to charity in 2005, he was actually criticized by some liberal bloggers for getting too much of a tax deduction. Congress had temporarily changed normal IRS rules that cap charitable contribution tax deductions at 50 percent. No prominent liberal politician seemed to run into the same problem.

But charity is not just a function of giving. It's also a question of who you give to. The liberal conceit has been that they are concerned about the less fortunate, the poor and vulnerable. But charitable organizations in the United States run the gamut from churches, poverty groups, think tanks, and lobbies to symphonies, colleges, and universities. And when it comes to charitable organizations, liberals often opt to give to toney cultural organizations rather than to poverty groups. Conservatives on the other hand give to organizations that *directly aid* the less fortunate.

Consider the cases of Democrat House Speaker Nancy Pelosi and radio talk show host Rush Limbaugh. Pelosi has long been outspoken on the need to help the poor. She has lambasted Republicans for "turning a deaf ear" to the problem.[21] On other occasions she has claimed that Republicans have launched "a shameful attack on the poor" and denounced conservatives as "hurting those who need our help most."[22] She explained at one point, "It is an act of worship to minister to the needs of the world's poorest."[23]

But Pelosi's "acts of worship" apparently do not involve her own resources. Pelosi and her husband Paul have established a charitable foundation (the Pelosi Family Foundation) to give to the causes they want to support. According to the charity's tax returns from 2001 to 2006, the Pelosis have donated hundreds of thousands over the past decade to numerous charitable organizations. Listed on the tax form are contributions to the San Francisco Museum of Modern Art ($36,500), the San Francisco Symphony ($5,600), and Georgetown University ($25,000). There was even money given to elite prep schools like the Town School for Boys in San Francisco and for an animal rights organization. These are causes that play well among the elite liberals who make large campaign donations. But the poor (who rarely vote in large numbers) were out of luck. With the exception of an occasional thousand-dollar donation to a Boys and Girls Club, little went to help the less fortunate (unless you count starving artists and kids at prep school).[24]

Pelosi is not alone. Many liberals who lecture about the need for greater compassion fail to give anything to the poor. Barbra Streisand likes to criticize conservatives for being selfish and greedy, unconcerned about the less fortunate. On her album *My Name Is Barbra* she even includes a "Poverty Medley," which includes a number of "down and out" songs. For a filmed version of the album, Streisand sang the medley in New York's Bergdorf's department store to dramatize her point.

Every year Streisand gives away large sums of money to charitable organizations through the Barbra Streisand Foundation. Amazingly, however, very little of it actually goes to the needy. The largest recipients in recent years have included well-heeled environmental groups, the ACLU, the Bill Clinton Foundation, Media Matters, and People for the American Way. These are all groups that hire professionals to advocate on particular policy positions. Streisand is certainly free to do this, but what's striking is how little of the money she gives to charity ends up in the hands of the less fortunate. To the extent that Streisand gives to organizations that are involved in poverty issues, these are organizations such as the Institute for America's Future, which *talk* about alleviating poverty while advocating higher taxes. But they don't actually feed a single person (except for their employees).[25]

Filmmaker Michael Moore, tribune of the downtrodden

masses, falls into the same category. He has a charitable foundation and gives away tens of thousands of dollars every year. But according to tax returns filed with the IRS, his poverty-fighting efforts are largely limited to supporting Lincoln Center, the Ann Arbor Film Festival, and other artsy forums. In the most recent year with tax records available (2005), Moore gave grants to six students who raised money for him to come speak at Cal State San Marcos. These scholarships of $2,500 apiece to six students don't even cover half of his speaking fee.[26]

Some on the left defend this practice of giving largely to the arts. Garrison Keillor argues that funding the arts is essential because "art speaks for the powerless."[27] While that sort of thinking no doubt appeals to the performance artist trying to make a go of it in San Francisco, it's doubtful that you will find many of the poor of the Mississippi Delta or Chicago's South Side in agreement. To them it looks like welfare for middle-class kids who would rather not go to law school.

Not all liberal philanthropists fall into this category, of course. The actor Paul Newman, through his product line Newman's Own, gives large sums of money to charities, almost all of it to serve the disadvantaged. The list of recipients includes ill children and programs for the elderly and the handicapped. Moreover, Newman is not preaching his compassion for all to see. He rarely lectures other people about being more generous. He's simply out there doing it himself.

Now contrast the charitable giving of Nancy Pelosi with

that of a conservative such as Rush Limbaugh. The talk show host has been called "heartless," "uncaring," and "cruel" by his liberal critics. But in contrast to Pelosi and her ilk, Limbaugh actually gives charitably to the needy. He has given millions to such causes as the Marine Corps–Law Enforcement Foundation, which gives money to the children of Marines and law enforcement agents who die on active duty, and the Leukemia & Lymphoma Society. And he supports other causes as well. According to charitable tax filings with the IRS, in one year Limbaugh gave $109,716 to "various individuals in need of assistance mainly due to family illnesses," $52,898 to "children's case management organizations" including "various programs to benefit families in need," $35,100 for "Alzheimer's community care—day care for families in need," and $40,951 for air-conditioning units and heaters delivered to troops in Iraq. For some reason, the San Francisco Museum of Modern Art did not make the list.[28]

You find a similar pattern with other conservatives. Among George W. Bush's favorite charities you find the Salvation Army and the Red Cross; Bill O'Reilly's include the Haitian Health Foundation, Father Joe's Villages (for the homeless), Best Friends (for inner-city children), and Habitat for Humanity. No elite prep schools made the list. This gap is not just present among certain celebrities or media elites. American businessmen are often upbraided by liberal journalists for their greedy pursuit of money and lack of social concern. But when scholars at Smith College looked into who was actually volunteering for charitable organizations, they came to a startling conclusion: Business leaders were spending almost twice as much time doing just that compared to journalists.[29]

Nor is this practice limited to prominent liberals. Rank-and-file liberals fall into the same self-satisfied charity gap: proclaiming their solidarity with the poor while actually doing less to help them than conservatives. Instead, advocacy for liberal policies is seen as a substitute for directly helping the poor. Why not do both?

Apparently what modern liberals like is feeling solidarity and compassion for the poor. Liberals are often "friends of goodness," but fall woefully short when it comes to doing any actual good. The American National Election Survey asked people whether they felt "close" to certain groups—the rich, the poor, businessmen, and so on. Even though liberals had the same income as conservative respondents, for some reason 74 percent of liberals claimed to "feel close" to poor people. Only 15 percent said they "felt close to businesspeople." Garrison Keillor expresses this attitude perfectly when he explains that liberals "begin with sympathy for the helpless." But liberalism often *ends* there as well. This is because modern liberalism is more about feelings than actions. These fine sentiments do nothing to assist the helpless, but nonetheless leave those on the left feeling self-satisfied about their attitudes.

When asked whether people should help others less fortunate, more than 93 percent of "strong Democrats" agreed with that statement, compared with 89 percent of "strong

Republicans." Not a big difference there. But when the survey asked, "Have you given money to a charity in the last year?"—25 percent of those "strong Democrats" said no. Another 50 percent said they had given only two to three times in the last year.[30]

Over the past fifteen years, the General Social Survey has consistently shown that religious conservatives are 25 percentage points more likely than liberals to donate money to help the poor and are 23 points more likely to volunteer time for that cause. As Arthur Brooks points out, the annual gap in giving is large: $2,210 for religious conservatives, $642 for skinflint liberals.[31]

Another study found that conservatives were much more likely to volunteer their time to a charity. The survey found that 30 percent of conservatives had donated time to a church, compared with only 12 percent of liberals. Even with nonchurch charities conservatives have an edge: 27 percent of conservatives volunteered for nonchurch charities compared to 19 percent of liberals.[32]

When asked by still another study "Have you given money to charity?"—strong Democrats were more than twice as likely to say they had not in the past year compared to strong Republicans. In contrast, Republicans were three times as likely to say that they had given to charity at least once a week when compared to strong Democrats.[33]

When asked "Did you do volunteer work last year?"—44 percent of conservatives said yes compared to 39 percent of liberals. Entirely satisfied with their attitude of solidarity toward the poor, liberals apparently didn't feel the need to help them in person. One wonders how they can feel so "close" to the poor given that they rarely spend any time with them. "Feeling close" to the poor while actually doing very little for them is a form of psychological self-satisfaction that does nothing other than help liberals feel good.

Among young people you find a similar trend. Young conservatives were more likely to volunteer for a charity, any type of charity, than young liberals. On the other hand, young liberals were more likely to say that they had attended a protest rally.[34]

Claiming sympathy for the poor while actually doing very little for them is a widespread phenomenon on the left. That is because liberals confuse activism with genuine action. Ralph Nader, for example, has spoken for years about the horrors of poverty and the responsibility that prosperous Americans bear for helping them. But Nader himself has given little to help those in poverty. All of his charitable contributions go to his own charities, where his employees are paid to advocate for the poor. Needless to say, none of this charity ends up in the hands of the poor. Nader actually has a rather low opinion of charity for the poor. As he puts it: "A society that has more justice is a society that needs less charity." Much better to have the government redistribute the wealth.

Consider the case of Jesse Jackson, who has for three decades attacked conservatives and regular Americans as heartless and failing to show adequate concern for the poor.

Jackson has claimed that he operates from a "liberal spirit of compassion and love," while conservatives are "heartless and uncaring toward the silent poor." He has created a sympathy empire that feeds off the generosity or guilt of others, and he has made quite a living from the business ventures that have resulted from his activities. In the 1980s, for example, he was making more than $200,000 a year but donated less than 1 percent of his income to charity.[35]

In addition to his nonprofit activist organizations, Jackson and his family have created a charity that is designed to express their support for the underprivileged. The Jackson Foundation receives large corporate donations every year, and the board is controlled exclusively by Jackson family members. In 2004, IRS records indicate that the family took in close to a million dollars from corporations like McDonald's, Anheuser-Busch, Alabama Power, GMAC, and several large law firms. When asked by the IRS to describe "direct charitable activities," the foundation responded: "None." From the $964,000 collected that year in donations, the Jackson Foundation donated a mere $46,000 to a couple of colleges. It spent nearly twice that amount—$84,172—on a "gala celebration" in honor of . . . Jesse Jackson.[36]

Multimillionairess Arianna Huffington, a onetime conservative pundit who now pontificates from the left, is another prominent liberal who is quick to label conservatives as unconcerned about the poor. They have "shamelessly abandoned the poor," she has written. In her book *Fanatics and Fools,* Huffington created what she called a compassion index, condemning wealthy individuals who give to charity and don't support the causes she does: "I found out firsthand that it's much easier to raise money for fashionable cultural causes and prestigious educational institutions than for homeless shelters and mentoring programs for at-risk children. The annual $3,500-a-plate, black-tie ball for the Costume Institute of the Metropolitan Museum of Art raises enough money to buy plenty of warm winter coats for children in New York City. But instead the funds go to preserving and displaying the evening gowns of the social elite."

Given such acerbic (and well-aimed) comments, one would expect Huffington to be a great benefactor of those in poverty. But when she released her tax returns in 2003 during a run for California governor, it was quickly revealed that she actually made no contributions to charities helping the poor and destitute. Her contributions ($6,675) went almost exclusively to the Church of the Movement of Inner Spiritual Awareness, a Hollywood-based New Age cult catering to starlets and the wealthy.

The myth that conservatives are selfish and liberals altruistic is so ingrained in our thinking that many researchers are stunned when they find the opposite to be true. For years the Harvard psychiatry department has conducted the Harvard Study of Adult Development. With a sample of 268 Harvard sophomores, they have attempted to evaluate various personality traits. Psychiatry professor George Vaillant, a lifelong Democrat, was surprised by the results. "I certainly had all kinds of prejudices, and doing the study got me to change them," he told *Harvard* magazine. "I thought that the Democrats would be a whole lot nicer and more altruistic, and that wasn't the case at all." What he did find, however, is that the Democrats were more "thin-skinned" than the Republicans.[37]

It shouldn't be surprising that, unlike the nursery study out of Berkeley that purported to show how whiny conservatives are, Vaillant's results have not received any attention from the mainstream media.

What is true of liberals as individuals also tends to be true of liberal communities. A few years ago, several community foundations around the country, in conjunction with Harvard University, conducted a massive study titled the Social Capital Community Benchmark Survey to determine how connected people are with each other and how much they give back to their communities. In all, they surveyed more than thirty thousand people. What they discovered is that liberal communities are actually terrible when it comes to helping others. The study speaks volumes about the state of modern liberalism.

San Francisco prides itself on being supportive of the less fortunate. It has roughly the same number of homeless people that New York does, but only one-tenth the population. The homeless receive generous cash payments and little attention from law enforcement. "Here," noted the *Christian Science Monitor,* "urinating in public is a cherished right."[38] Recently, when the city wanted to displace some homeless people from the wealthy Corona Heights neighborhood because of complaints by residents, they dealt with the problem indirectly—bringing in hungry goats to munch away at the thick brush to prevent the homeless from finding a quiet place to sleep in the park.[39]

But how does San Francisco stack up in an objective study of American cities?

Using a "giving and volunteering" index, the Benchmark study measured how much time residents volunteered for charity and how much money they donated. With 100 being the average national score, liberal San Francisco received a 79, Boston (and equally liberal Cleveland) a 77. In other words, they were near the bottom of the scale. In the Minnesota Twin Cities, more liberal north Minneapolis received a slightly below average 95, while more conservative St. Paul was rated an above-average 112. Boulder, Colorado, home of radical professor Ward Churchill and other self-styled progressive academics, received a below-average 90. In contrast, more conservative Winston-Salem, North Carolina, received a 123, as did nearby Greensboro. Red state South Dakota scored 127, conservative Charlotte 125.[40]

The Catalogue for Philanthropy tried a different approach, but came to the same conclusion. Comparing each state's average itemized charitable deductions with its average adjusted gross income (based on IRS data), the study found that 28 of the 29 "most generous" states are red states that voted for President Bush (including all 25 of the "most generous" states), while 17 of the 21 "least generous" are blue states that voted for Senator Kerry (including all 7 of the "least generous"). When they went back a few years earlier, they found that liberals did no better with Bill Clinton in power. Of the 10 lowest-giving states, 9 voted for Bill Clinton in 1996. Of the highest-giving states, 8 voted for Republican nominee Bob Dole.

Why are liberals such stingy givers when they profess to have so much concern about the poor? Why are liberal communities less hospitable to the poor than conservative ones? Part of the explanation is that the left has adopted a worldview that tells them they can make little difference in the world as individuals. Despite their idealized view of grassroots social movements, today's liberals seem to have concluded (perhaps from the example of the civil rights movement) that only the government can really change things. A revealing study conducted by the Center for Democracy and Citizenship found that a majority of conservative Republicans believe they individually can help solve problems in our country while only 28 percent of liberal Democrats shared that view. Liberalism promotes the idea that government solutions are the best solutions, which has the effect not only of encouraging government growth but also discouraging a sense of individual empowerment.

Another important difference is that conservatives emphasize action when tackling problems, while liberals emphasize discussion. Professor Bruce Fleming, an unabashed liberal teaching at the decidedly conservative U.S. Naval Academy, has noticed the differences over the years between his largely conservative students and his liberal friends. "Conservatism is about things done, not things said," he writes. "Liberalism, by contrast, is all about articulating your own position with respect to someone else's. It's about words." This makes sense given that liberals tend to give to organizations that discuss social problems while conservatives give to charities that tackle them directly.[41]

Consider the difference between the Walton Family Foundation, managed by the largely conservative heirs of Wal-Mart founder Sam Walton, and the charitable activities of über-liberal George Soros. Both charities have given away enormous sums of money. But the Walton Family Foundation has given the bulk of its contributions to building schools, funding charter schools in poverty-stricken areas, scholarship funds, and practical solutions for the underclass. Soros on the other hand has given millions to advocates for his policy views: higher taxes, drug legalization, and environmentalism. In short, Soros tends to talk about problems; the Waltons have set about fixing them.

Liberals may "feel" that they are close to the poor and express that idea to others. But conservatives are actually more likely to help the poor. As Fleming explains, "A liberal is perfectly capable of saying that he or she should do something and yet will not do so; the conservative . . . is already moving as soon as the word 'should' is pronounced."[42]

Liberals by and large are content to believe that "good intentions" are all that matter. But good intentions are nothing by themselves. Margaret Thatcher captured this difference perfectly when she explained, "No one would remember the Good Samaritan if he'd only had good intentions—he had money, too."

Liberals also embrace an "I gave at the office" mentality. Because they believe it's the government's responsibility to solve the problem of poverty, and have voted and even campaigned for liberal candidates, they believe they have done their bit to alleviate poverty. Surveys confirm that the more strongly someone espouses the view that the government should equalize income in the United States, the more likely they are *not* to give to charity. As Professor James Lindgren of the Northwestern University School of Law points out, "Those who oppose more government distribution of income were much more likely to donate money to charities. . . . those who wanted the government to promote income leveling were less likely to be generous themselves."[43]

Adam Smith, the eighteenth-century founder of laissez-faire economics, was famous for his charitable pursuits, often quietly and anonymously giving money to the less fortunate. According to his biographer, when Smith died, he had very little money even though he had made quite a fortune in his day. The reason? "He had given away generous sums from his income in secret to charity."[44] In contrast, his great philosophical nemesis, Karl Marx, the tribune of the workingman, was a miserly individual who gave little if anything to the poor. As with others on the left, helping the poor is limited to the plane of abstract notions about how to reorganize society to meet their needs. The actual poor of the here and now reap no benefit from these grandiose plans.

Nor will they. For the main point of liberal compassion appears to be making liberals themselves feel good about their superior virtue. Such are the rewards of being a "friend of goodness."

LIBERAL$ AND MONEY
Or, Why Liberals Are More Envious and Less Hardworking Than Conservatives

I n 1995, then First Lady Hillary Clinton traveled to Pakistan as part of a five-country goodwill mission to South Asia. She visited a hospital, met with leaders, and talked to young girls at a school. In the small village of Burki, outside Lahore, she stood in front of poor young girls and gave a short talk about how "rampant materialism and consumerism" are widespread in the West. She warned the girls that the same thing might soon threaten their own country. No doubt many in the audience wished that it *would.*[1]

A few years later, in the waning months of her husband's

presidency, Mrs. Clinton blasted what she called "a consumer-driven culture that promotes values that undermine democracy" and "materialism that undermines our spiritual centers." Days after the Clintons left the White House, they signed $20 million in book contracts, bought two multimillion-dollar homes, and added a beachfront property in the Dominican Republic. Meanwhile, the former president hit the lecture circuit and raked in $40 million in six years, according to the *Washington Post*.[2]

Still, she insisted, "We're not about money."

Billionaire Ted Turner took his father's outdoor advertising company and through aggressive acquisitions, hardfisted financial dealings, a decidedly antiunion attitude, and an incredible desire to win, turned it into one of the largest media companies in the world. Along the way Turner has become the largest landowner in the world, with enormous ranches in Argentina, New Mexico, Florida, Montana, and Texas. He owns aircraft, boats, and an extensive art collection.

But according to Turner, this does not make him a capitalist. At the Time-Warner Conference in Shanghai, he told the audience that he was, in fact, a "socialist at heart." On his first date with Jane Fonda, he explained, "some of my best friends are communists." He has praised Fidel Castro and blasted fellow corporate executives for conspicuous consumption. Turner complains that wealth creation in America has become too easy. Some in the high-tech sector are making "too much money too fast."

When liberals complain that some people are making

"too much" money, they are usually talking about *other people's* money. Turner may be a socialist "at heart," but he clearly doesn't want to take things too far. In 2002 he gave an impassioned talk at his alma mater, Brown University, in which he described himself as an idealist who wanted to save the world. He even compared himself to Paul Revere. But when a student from Montana stood and asked Turner to open up his large ranch in that state to the general public, he got visibly angry. "We still believe in private property in this country," groused the billionaire socialist.[3]

Hillary Clinton and Ted Turner are not the only modern liberals who, in the words of former *New York Times* columnist Daniel Akst, are bent on saving the rest of us from the horrors of consumption while working aggressively to acquire and consume as much as they can themselves. Michael Moore has made tens of millions in the film business as a producer and director. All the while he has complained strenuously that corporate CEOs are "rip-off artists" because they make much more than the average American worker. But Moore himself makes enormous sums compared to others in his industry. In the same year that he banked tens of millions from *Fahrenheit 9/11,* the average member of the Screen Actors Guild made only $5,000, according to the Bureau of Labor Statistics. The average earnings of a film producer in that year were $52,840. Yet Moore never complains about the income and earning disparities in his own industry. Still less does he do anything about it.

Former senator and presidential candidate John Edwards

has talked for years about the "two Americas" of rich and poor. A major cause of this disparity, according to him, is the fact that the economy benefits "wealthy insiders" who evade taxes and don't pay their fair share. But he undoubtedly did not mean to include the private trust he established for his family to avoid paying an inheritance tax. Nor did he have in mind the Fortress Investment Group, a hedge fund for which he was an adviser and is also an investor. The fund is not incorporated in the United States but in the Cayman Islands, which allows investors and partners to defer or avoid paying U.S. taxes. Why on earth would he want to do that?

Modern liberals are obsessed with how much other people have, how much they spend, how they spend it, and what they plan to do with it. Thus Bryant Gumbel complained in the 1990s that Internet entrepreneurs were motivated by "greed," while he was being paid $5 million a year. (Obviously, greed and avarice were not a factor in his contract negotiations with CBS.) Likewise, talk show host and liberal extraordinaire Rosie O'Donnell complained in 2000 that her neighbors in Greenwich, Connecticut, "have too much money." (Rosie has never been quoted as saying that *she* has too much money.)[4] During the Internet boom of the nineties, Labor Secretary Robert Reich suggested that people who were making so much money should be willing to give more to the government. "Give me more money and I'll find more uses," he quipped.[5]

Many on the left certainly believe that those who have made money don't necessarily know how to best spend it.

When America faced a federal budget surplus in the nineties, President Clinton was asked whether he would be proposing any tax cuts. "We could give it all back to you and hope you spend it right," he said. "But . . . if you don't spend it *right,* here's what's going to happen," and he went on to list a litany of horrors. Not surprisingly, Clinton has never expressed the view that his own money should be subject to government control to make sure it is spent correctly. Clinton has repeatedly said that he has benefited from President George W. Bush's tax cut, but that he really shouldn't because he's already very wealthy. But he never returns the money to the IRS as he certainly could do at any time.[6]

Perhaps no subject creates so much angst, confusion, and contradiction for modern liberals as money. They profess to dislike excessive consumption, greed, and income inequality. Those, after all, are the vices of conservatives. The late John Kenneth Galbraith, the esteemed Harvard economist, perfectly captured this haughty attitude when he defined conservative thinking as an effort to make "greed respectable." Anthony Lewis, former columnist for the *New York Times*, has likewise scolded conservatives and capitalists in general for believing that "money is the measure of all things." Billionaire George Soros (when he's not busy speculating on currency swings) dismisses those less predatory than himself as motivated by greed because they want to abolish the inheritance tax. Former congressman Jim Weaver (D-OR) claims that greed is literally hardwired into conservatives; it is part of their genetic makeup. Conservatives, he writes, manifestly have a "lesser awareness of other people's plight," while liberals have "greater empathy toward others" and are less acquisitive.[7] A popular T-shirt for sale on the Internet says it all: "Liberals love people. Conservatives love money."

Those on the political left are absolutely convinced that they are less materialistic and more altruistic than conservatives. Talk show host Alan Colmes has argued that "Jesus was a liberal" because he was much more generous with his limited resources than a conservative would be. As Ben Wattenberg has put it, "The word 'conservative' conjures up images of the miserly Ebenezer Scrooge, while 'liberal' brings to mind kindly Santa Claus."

The media has perpetuated this idea for years. During the 1980s the American economy grew briskly under Ronald Reagan. A few years later, NBC's Katie Couric assured her viewers that in the Reagan era, "greed and materialism was the norm." Couric's was just one voice in a media chorus that saw Reagan's theory of "trickle-down economics" as a cynical expression of conservative selfishness and greed. But during the high-flying Internet bubble years of the Clinton administration, when the stock market was booming and instant millionaires and sky-high IPOs were the norm, there was no moralistic breastbeating in the media about how the Democrats had ushered in an era of untrammeled greed. More recently, *Good Morning America* cohost Charlie Gibson pushed this line when he dismissed the term "compassionate conservative" as a sham. After all, Gibson said, the phrase features the "juxtaposition of two seemingly contradictory terms."

The fact that conservatives are more interested in money than in higher pursuits is believed to explain a lot of things, including the lack of conservative professors on college campuses. The sparse number of conservative professors supposedly springs from conservative greed; they are simply not willing to take an academic job that pays less than the private sector. Duke University political science professor Samantha Luks says that teaching requires "the type of personality that would be willing to take a pay cut to do a certain type of work he or she deems important," and according to her, that individual is "more likely to vote Democratic." A college newspaper editorialized that liberals populate the faculty lounge because academic jobs "are more likely to appeal to people who are anti-materialistic and idealistic—in other words, liberals."[8]

But this mythology about greedy conservatives and altruistic liberals has no basis in fact. Indeed, the reality is quite the reverse. Time after time, reputable surveys show that liberals are more interested in money, think about it more often, and value it more highly than conservatives. They also feel less constrained about how they acquire it. Many liberals apparently believe that espousing liberal ideals is a "get out of jail free" card that inoculates them from the evils of the money culture.

Convinced that they are not overly interested in money or possessions, they are free to acquire them. It creates a bizarre set of attitudes whereby liberals are more likely to denounce money, but also more eager to pursue it.

Consider these numbers from the World Values Survey and the General Social Survey:

When asked if "high income" is very important in a job, 36 percent of those who call themselves "very liberal" said yes, compared with just 24 percent who said they were very conservative.

When asked whether they "aspire to be rich," liberals actually said yes 61 percent of the time, compared to 51 percent of conservatives.[9]

When asked whether "after good health, money is the most important thing," liberals agreed with that statement more than conservatives did, putting money ahead of family and friends (and apparently saving the planet).

Is money more important than life itself? A sizable number of liberals believe it is. When asked, Is it morally defensible to commit suicide if you are financially bankrupt?, those who describe themselves as very liberal were three times as likely to say yes compared to those who were very conservative (23 percent to 7 percent).

Does anything go when it comes to making money? When asked about the statement, "There are no right or wrong ways to make money," liberals were more likely to agree than conservatives.

The plain fact is that liberals value money more than conservatives in many respects. Liberals are more likely to haggle with a business owner to get a better price: 43 percent of liberals in one survey said they had done so, compared with only 32 percent of conservatives. Indeed, the farther left you go on the spectrum of those who disavow having an interest in money, the more willing they are to argue for a lower price. A whopping 67 percent of those who called themselves "extremely liberal" had tried to cut the price of an item for sale in a store. This is not, I hasten to add, because liberals are poor.

Those who are strong Democrats are also more likely (60 percent to 47 percent) to say they do not return money after getting too much change from a cashier.[10]

Many on the left spend an inordinate amount of time complaining about their financial lot in life. Conservatives were three times more likely to say that they were "satisfied" with their financial lot than liberals. Nor is this a case of poor, idealistic liberals being compared to rich and comfortable conservatives. Even when liberals and conservatives earn the *same income,* the results remain the same: Liberals are much more likely to be chronically dissatisfied with their financial situation.

Yet at the same time, the World Values Survey reveals that those on the left believe there needs to be "less emphasis on money" in our society. By more than 10 percentage points they agree with that sentiment when compared with political conservatives.[11] This myopic view of money and wealth is caused in large part by the skewed view many liberals have of how it is actually created. For many Americans, the American Dream is really about the Protestant Work Ethic: work hard, be frugal, get a good education, keep your nose clean, and you will be all right.

But that notion is rejected by a large number of liberals today. They see very little connection between diligence, effort, and wealth. Congressman Richard Gephardt argued a few years back that the wealthiest and most successful Americans were simply those who had "won the lottery of life." Their wealth was mainly a result of sheer luck. It had nothing to do with hard work, frugality, or being an entrepreneur who takes risks. (Curiously, the phrase "lottery of life" was first used by the grim economist Thomas Malthus, who falsely predicted worldwide famine as a result of population outstripping food production.) The late Molly Ivins went even further, arguing not only that life was a lottery, but that "Republicans have rigged it." Sen. John Edwards has likewise told people on the campaign trail that "our system rewards wealth, not work."

Michael Moore regularly tells those who will listen to him (sadly there are millions) that working hard to get ahead is foolish. In his book *Dude, Where's My Country?* he titles one chapter "Horatio Alger Must Die." Alger, the author of numerous books that exalt the ideal of the self-made man, promotes a "seductive myth," says Moore. It's a delusion to think that you can get wealthy through hard work. "The American carrot is dangled in front of us all our lives and we believe that we are almost within reach of making it," he writes. This is ridiculous, he says, and complains that "the system is rigged in favor of the few, and your name is not among them, not now and not ever."[12] (Of course, not only has the number of new millionaires in this country increased dramatically in recent decades, but Moore himself is living proof that hard work can make you rich—even if said work involves producing propaganda-laden films and exploiting underpaid workers.) Moore has actually embraced the so-called slacker culture of directionless, unmotivated young people as a thing to be admired. In 2004 he embarked on a "Slacker uprising tour" of college campuses.

French economist and author Corinne Maier wrote a bestselling book called *Bonjour Laziness,* which explained "why it is in your best interest to work as little as possible." Maier's sprightly attack on the capitalist work ethic has been published in nineteen countries. The *New York Times* proclaimed her "a countercultural heroine," and the book has been praised by the lefty *Village Voice,* explaining that it offers "practical suggestions for subverting the workplace." As if that were a fun, cool thing that everyone should do—as opposed to supporting our families and putting our children through school.

Some liberal education experts consider promoting hard work as a virtue to be part of a "profoundly conservative, if not reactionary, agenda." So says Alfie Kohn, a lecturer at education conferences around the country. Affiliated with the

Orwellian-sounding Greater Good Science Center, Kohn's work has been praised by Noam Chomsky and child psychologist Benjamin Spock. Enough said![13]

Nicholas von Hoffman, an unusually smug columnist at the *New York Observer*, shows utter disdain for the notion that hard work is a good thing. "In most circles, the highest compliment you can pay someone is to say that so-and-so has a good work ethic or a blue-collar mentality. Never mind that the person is dumb as a post." The American motto, he says, is "work hard, work stupid."[14]

But it's not just economic populists like Michael Moore and John Edwards, or writers like von Hoffman who show disdain for the traditional work ethic. Academics on the left, like Professor Peter Edelman of Georgetown University, a Clinton administration adviser, and Kenneth Keniston of Yale, have for years painted a picture of the American economy in which hard work really does not make any difference. In their view, only a fool would think such a thing. America is a "caste system," they claimed in one report, and most people face a "stacked deck." According to them it is simply ridiculous "to believe that any child with enough guts and ability can escape poverty and make a rewarding life."[15]

When liberal-centrists like Mickey Kaus (author of the widely praised *The End of Equality*) pushed the idea that a work ethic is essential to help the poor get out of poverty, he was criticized by colleagues on the left. Welfare reform, which would encourage those receiving government assistance to work, was likewise attacked because it would "force welfare mothers into slavery," as one critic put it.[16]

This attitude is widely accepted on the political left today. An extensive survey by the Pew Research Center found that *three out of four Republicans* believe that people can get ahead by working hard. *Four out of five* believe that everyone has the power to succeed. But Democrats have much less faith in the value of hard work. *Only 14 percent believe that people can get ahead by working hard,* according to the survey. And only 44 percent believe that everyone has the power to succeed. This is not a case of "rich" Republicans believing one thing and "poor" Democrats another. Even when you compare Republicans and Democrats of the *same income,* the gap still exists.

What this means is that many modern liberals believe differences in wealth are a result of dumb luck rather than hard work and a diligent attitude. It should therefore not be surprising that according to one scientific survey, liberals are *two and a half times* as likely to play the lottery or gamble in the hope of getting rich.[17]

Let's acknowledge that too many Americans are still being born into poverty and that they face tremendous odds in terms of obtaining the basic education and other support they need to rise higher in society. It does these people little good to preach that all they need to do is work a little harder, or to suggest that their problems are due to their own deficient moral virtue. Many times in life, hard work is not rewarded. Life is often unfair, and for some people the deck is indeed stacked greatly against them. But it harms such people even more to promote the view that no amount of effort on their part can ever change their circumstances, and that (in effect) they might as well give up. The fashionable cynicism on the left that sees America as a "caste system" is an absurd distortion of reality and does a deep disservice to those at the bottom of our society because it basically tells them to stop trying. That is a sure recipe for perpetuating their misfortunes.

Because the modern left does not see a connection between work and wealth, they are also much more willing to accept something for nothing. According to the World Values Survey, those who consider themselves conservatives were three times more likely to say it would be "humiliating" to receive money without having to work for it (as charity, unemployment, or welfare) when compared to those on the left. The survey also found that those on the left were much more likely to say it was justified to keep money that you found—even if it doesn't belong to you.

Using the highly regarded Mirels-Garrett Protestant Work Ethic Scale, professors Thomas Tang and Jen Tzeng conducted a massive study including 689 people and found that there was a definite correlation to conservative political views. Another study published in the *Journal of Social Psychology* found that a "strong correlation" exists between being conservative and working hard.[18] In Great Britain, researchers found that those who voted Conservative most embraced the hard work ethic, followed by Labor supporters. Marxists came out the laziest.[19] There are more than a dozen studies that confirm a link between conservative values and a strong work ethic. I have yet to find a single one that links a hard work ethic with liberalism.

Why is this important? Because the Protestant work ethic has been shown repeatedly to predict that people will work harder, be more motivated, and be more satisfied with their job and life in general.[20] Those who embrace the conservative work ethic "produce significantly more output on the job" than those who don't, "resist the temptation to cheat" on the job, and "persevere" when confronted with difficult challenges.[21] So the next time a guy shows up for an interview sporting a Che Guevara T-shirt and a résumé, you might want to think long and hard before you hire him.

Perhaps it is simple coincidence, but some of the biggest leftists in history have possessed the poorest work habits. Karl Marx lived on his father's money, and when that ran out he mooched funds from his mother. When that was gone he migrated to an uncle's pocketbook and then to his wife's family. Throughout his life he refused to get a job. His family became so poor that his wife and children were enfeebled by hunger and lacked medical attention. He finally tried to get a job as a railway clerk but was turned down. (He apparently had poor handwriting.) Ultimately he subsisted on money given to him by his wealthy friend Friedrich Engels until the day he died.

Socialist playwright George Bernard Shaw bragged to his friends that his mother supported him until he was thirty, as he wrote unpublished novels and strolled through the British Museum during the middle of the day idly looking at paintings.[22]

The problem is compounded by the rise of what political scientist Michael Barone calls "trust fund liberals," who have become a prominent feature on the political landscape today. Barone writes: "Who are the trustfunders? People with enough money not to have to work for a living, or not to have to work very hard. People who can live more or less wherever they want. . . . These people tend to be very liberal politically. Aware that they have done nothing to earn their money, they feel a certain sense of guilt." Barone, editor of the *Almanac of American Politics,* pointedly surveys their growing influence: "Not scattered randomly around the country, but heavily concentrated in certain areas . . . Trustfunders stand out even more vividly when you look at the political map of the Rocky Mountain states. In Idaho and Wyoming, each state's wealthiest county was also the only county to vote for John Kerry. . . . Massachusetts Catholics gave their fellow Massachusetts Catholic Kerry only 51 percent of their votes, but he won 77 percent in Boston, 85 percent in Cambridge, and 69 percent and 73 percent in trustfunder-heavy Hampshire and Berkshire Counties in the western mountains. . . ."

Shielded from the arduous demands of earning a living, trustfunders are equally shielded from the burdens of taxation through a variety of tax shelters, tax-free investments, and offshore accounts that less wealthy Americans simply cannot afford. Based on their own experience, trust-fund babies tend to view wealth as resulting from the lottery of life rather than something created by hard work. They assume everyone else who is rich got so through luck, like themselves.

It should also not come as a surprise that the two most fertile funding sites for liberal causes—Hollywood and the high-tech industry—reflect a similar disconnect. It's not that people don't work hard in Silicon Valley. But many of the high-tech millionaires and billionaires made their money quickly in IPOs fueled by what one economist has called "irrational exuberance." Some are worth billions after having worked just a few years in the field. Likewise in Hollywood, stars such as Johnny Depp became fabulously wealthy quite young and are now making $20 million or more for six weeks on a studio set. Unlike the entrepreneur who amassed a fortune over decades of struggle and sacrifice, these liberal "instant rich" are not likely to have the same appreciation for long, arduous work. In short, the Silicon Valley thirty-year-old worth $200 million after six years in the business is likely to have a different view of wealth accumulation than the industrialist who amassed a similar fortune over the course of a lifetime. In these gilded liberal Neverlands, wealth does seem less the result of hard work than the winnings from the lottery of life.

The point is not that people on the left are intrinsically bad or lazy, but that ideas influence behavior. And if your belief system tells you that hard work doesn't matter that much, you are unlikely to work very hard. When the General Social Survey asked: What is more important to you, work or leisure?—the results were predictable. Forty-two percent of those who were "very liberal" named leisure as more important. Only 15 percent of conservatives said the same. (Another survey found that in a given year, 26 percent of self-described liberals called in sick to work, compared to only 14 percent of conservatives.)

A study in the *Journal of Management Development* found that a desire for lots of leisure was negatively correlated with "general conservative beliefs."[23]

The left also doesn't like the idea of competition. When asked if competition is good, those who defined themselves as very liberal said yes only 14 percent of the time. Conservatives said competition was good 43 percent of the time.

What those on the left believe about money and work also influences how they think about their jobs. Asked by the General Social Survey to rank the five attributes they would prefer in a job, both liberals and conservatives ranked "gives a feeling of accomplishment" first. But conservatives ranked it much higher than liberals. In second place for those on the left was a "high-income" job, while for conservatives the second spot was "chances for advancement." Liberals picked "working hours are short, lots of free time" well ahead of conservatives. Liberals were also much more likely to pick "high income" as the most important factor in selecting a job: 26 percent of liberals compared to 19 percent of conservatives. Surprisingly as well (to liberals, that is), conservatives were more likely to list a job that was "useful to society"—58 to 50 percent.[24]

In another survey, broken down by party affiliation, Democrats were twice as likely to mention a job that "leaves time for leisure" when compared with Republicans.[25] Liberals mentioned they wanted a job with "no pressure" 56 percent of the time. Those who counted themselves conservative mentioned it only 36 percent of the time.

So we see the divide. Conservatives tend to choose jobs in which you can advance and achieve something. Those on the left, on the other hand, tend to prefer jobs with generous holidays, high pay, and good job security. (Who doesn't want a job like that?) These markedly different attitudes are highlighted when you compare the nonofficial activities of our recent political leaders. How have Ronald Reagan, Bill Clinton, John Kerry, Al Gore, and George W. Bush used their leisure time? Ronald Reagan famously worked hard at his ranch—fixing fences, tending to his horses, clearing brush. The stone patio in front of his ranch home was built by Reagan himself, and when the home needed reroofing, he did it with his own hands. He proudly showed off his handiwork to visitors like Mikhail Gorbachev. Likewise, George W. Bush has spent considerable time in Crawford, Texas, clearing brush, blazing trails, and repairing the barn. Bill Clinton, John Kerry, and Al Gore prefer to use their leisure time playing—jogging, socializing, shopping, sailing, skiing, and the like.

Some might argue that such activities are really just photo opportunities, designed to cast these figures in the most positive light. According to this view, Bush and Reagan worked on their ranches merely to convey an image—not because they felt obliged to be useful around the house. Even if you buy this cynical view—and there is plenty of evidence that it is wrong—it still makes the relevant point. Conservative political figures no doubt believe that demonstrating an ethic of hard work will send positive cues to their voters. Liberal constituents are not nearly so impressed.

None of this is to suggest that liberals don't work hard. Many of them certainly do. But in doing so they are rejecting the prevailing liberal economic philosophy. They are saying in effect that life is not a lottery and that hard work does pay off. That is a distinctly minority view on the left today.

Researchers at the University of California and Southern Illinois University asked more than 160 people of varying political beliefs how much they would be willing to help people who were facing economic difficulties. Each was given a pot of money with which they could help people in need. What they found is that liberals pretty much wanted to help *everyone*. Unrepentant drunks or loafers received the same support as those who had faced a medical problem or tragedy. Those who refused to work got the same as those who had suffered a temporary setback. In short, everyone got basically the same amount of help from liberals who participated. Conservatives on the other hand were willing to treat people differently—depending on whether they were willing to work. The end result was that conservatives were actually "more willing than liberals to provide government assistance to laid-off but dependable Black workers" precisely because they were willing to work. Liberals on the other hand tended to be mindlessly egalitarian, unwilling to make a distinction between those who behave irresponsibly and those who don't.[26]

The upshot is that modern liberals are blind to the link between effort and reward. If money is a function of luck and hard work does not really help you get ahead, then people are not responsible for their economic circumstances. Liberals therefore reject the notion of individual responsibility. Conservatives on the other hand are more supportive of those who are actually trying, even if they have faced a temporary setback.

The left's obsession with money is compounded by the fact that they measure equality in largely economic terms. When the *New York Times* produces statistics which demonstrate that the income gap is widening, the left is quick to declare this a bad thing. John Edwards has said that because of income inequality, "It's hard to call it the American Dream" anymore. Hillary Clinton has explained that we are "in the era of the Robber Barons."

Economic equality is seen by many on the left as essential to political and legal equality. What this means of course is that modern liberalism is preoccupied with material things as the measure of equality. Barry Goldwater recognized early on that for this reason, liberals are more money-obsessed than conservatives. "The error of liberals is that they concern themselves over much with material things," Goldwater once said. "Liberals regard the satisfaction of economic want as the dominant mission of society. They are, moreover, in a hurry." In contrast, Goldwater noted, "Conservatism looks upon the enhancement of man's spiritual nature as the primary concern of political philosophy."

Moreover, as one might expect, this focus on economic equality—particularly when it comes to other people's money—leads to the rise of the green-eyed monster: envy. Research shows that those on the political left are more resentful and envious than others. One study found that liberals were two and a half times more likely to say they were resentful of others' success. When asked to respond to the statement, "I have been jealous of others' good luck," liberals were 50 percent more likely to agree than conservatives.

Another study found that those on the left were even willing to give up money themselves if that would take more from those who had a greater amount. Scholars at Oxford and Warwick Universities decided to explore the concept of envy in a series of experiments. Setting up a computer game that allowed people to accumulate money, they gave participants the option to spend some of their own money in order to take away more from someone else. The result? Those who considered themselves "egalitarians" (i.e., left of center) were much more willing to give up some of their own money if it meant taking *more money* from someone else.[27]

Ralph Reiland, a professor at Robert Morris University, recalls a dispute between two of his students several years ago. Both took a job at a pizza place making $6.25 an hour. One student came up with a business idea and went to work making it happen. His first employee was his pizza shop coworker. The business was enormously successful. The employee went from making $6.25 an hour to $15 an hour. But the student who started the business was soon making $50 an hour. His friend soon quit and went back to making just $6.25 an hour at the pizza place. He thought it was "unfair" that his friend was making more.[28]

Another study from the University of London asked over 250 people how they used money as part of a belief and behavioral scale. Their findings: Those on the left were much more likely to have "used money as a source of power over people" than conservatives.[29]

The fact is that professed egalitarians—people who want to take from the rich and give to the poor—are generally a pretty miserable lot. Professor James Lindgren of the Northwestern University School of Law examined survey data and discovered that those who are strongly in favor of redistributing wealth are more unhappy and envious than those who do not. They are also more resentful, less tolerant of others, and more likely to possess racist views.[30]

None of this should come as a surprise, given the recent turn of modern liberal thought. For the vast expanse of human history, envy has been seen as a bad thing. According to Helmut Schoeck in his study *Envy*, all major religions have viewed envy as a sin, something to be avoided. Even primitive societies saw envy "as a disease, the envious man as dangerously sick—a cancer from which the individual and the group must be protected." The reason, says Schoeck, is that envy is destructive. "Just as the envious man does not wish to possess but merely to see destroyed the property he covets, he may begin by hurting himself—or at least by incurring unnecessary expenditure—simply in order to torment the man he envies."[31] Oliver Wendell Holmes understood this connection, writing in a letter to a friend, "I have no respect for the passion for [economic] equality, which seems to me merely idealizing envy. . . ."[32]

And yet modern liberalism has embraced envy as a measure for economic justice. Liberal thinker Ronald Dworkin believes that justice demands economic equality and argues that the only way to determine what is equal is the absence of envy. Dworkin calls this "the envy test." If envy exists, then injustice still exists. The problem, according to Schoeck, is that the more one embraces economic equality, the more one "will become increasingly envious as this principle becomes institutionalized." In short, economic "equality is, in fact, the expression of envy."

Envy may be considered a vice by many, but Dworkin and others have made it a cornerstone of their ethical thinking. Indeed, he considers envy to be a key component of his ideal society.[33]

This is not to say that conservatives can't be envious. But how you view someone else's success can strongly influence how you respond to it. Because conservatives tend to view success as the reward of hard work, they see it as the result of merit and character. Because those on the left see wealth accumulation more as a function of luck, they often regard it as something illegitimate that needs to be corrected. And they are often willing to harm themselves to do so.

4.

THE WHOLE TRUTH AND NOTHING BUT Or, Why Conservatives Value Honesty More Than Liberals

W ould you buy a used car from a family member? Would it matter if they happen to be liberal? These seem like ridiculous questions. You can trust a family member, can't you? And why would the politics of the person selling you a used car matter? The answers might surprise you.

Words like "honesty" and "lying" get tossed around a lot, particularly when it comes to politics. All politicians like to tell the truth selectively. But people seem to place a different value on whether honesty and truth-telling are important. Allan Bloom, in his book *The Closing of the American Mind,* wrote about the corrosive effects that relativism has on the search for truth. A large number of modern liberals don't even believe that "truth" exists. As Bloom put it, the new language of relativism says "one need not feel bad or uncomfortable with oneself when just a little value adjustment is necessary."[1] If truth is relative, then honesty is a subjective thing. As Sidney Hook once put it, "The easiest rationalization for the refusal to seek the truth is the denial that truth exists."[2]

In short, modern liberalism creates an atmosphere where lying becomes more acceptable. As a result, modern liberals are more comfortable with dishonesty and cheating.

For years, the highly respected World Values Survey has been asking thousands of Americans all sorts of questions about what they believe, particularly as it relates to questions of right and wrong. They often probe people with questions that pose an ethical dilemma. For example: If you were selling a used car to a family member, and the transmission wasn't working so well, would you tell them? Remarkably, nearly 20 percent of those who described themselves as very liberal said they would not tell a family member about the faulty transmission. (One marvels at the surprising honesty displayed by those who think that lying to a relative is okay.) In short, they were three times more likely than self-described conservatives to say it was acceptable to sell Aunt Betty a car with a bum transmission.[3]

Would you claim government benefits you were not entitled to if you could get away with it? The World Values Survey asked thousands of Americans that question. The results, again, were startling. Liberals were more than twice as likely as conservatives to say it is okay to get welfare benefits they were not entitled to. One-third of those who said they were very liberal said it was fine, compared to only 15 percent of conservatives.[4]

The National Cultural Values Survey asked a similar question. "You lose your job. Your friend's company is looking for someone to do temporary work. They are willing to pay the person in cash to avoid taxes and allow the person to still collect unemployment. What would you do?" Almost half (49 percent) of self-described progressives said they would take the job, cheating on their taxes and lying when collecting government benefits. Only 21 percent of conservatives said they would go along.[5]

Billionaire George Soros, a financial patron of numerous liberal/left causes, actually tried to do this very thing when he was younger. As a poor young man, Soros tried to get a Jewish charity to give him money while also receiving public assistance. When the charity refused, Soros was furious. This is ironic, since, as Joshua Muravchik points out, Soros was trying to perpetrate a fraud by double-dipping and not disclosing his pension. We know about this incident because Soros actually bragged about it in a series of interviews.[6]

Liberals consistently advocate for higher taxes and typically hold the view that many Americans, particularly those who are wealthy, should pay more. Such a view would seem to suggest that liberals abhor cheating on taxes, while conservatives, always grousing about the tax man, would be willing to cut a few fiscal corners. But the opposite is true: When the survey asked whether it was okay to cheat on one's taxes, 57 percent of those who described themselves as "very liberal" said it was all right. Of those who described themselves as "very conservative," only 20 percent said it was acceptable.[7]

Liberals often push for taxes on "moral grounds," but many don't see lying on their 1040 as an immoral act. A survey by the Pew Research Center found that 86 percent of conservatives considered it "morally wrong" to cheat on their taxes. Only 68 percent of liberals agreed.[8]

This laxity about paying taxes is not an abstraction to liberals. Gore Vidal, who has piously declared that "greed rules the American heart" and that the rich don't pay enough in taxes, once tried to claim his Jaguar sports car as a deductible expense. When the IRS challenged him, he claimed he was being persecuted.[9]

Rev. Al Sharpton is another prominent liberal who pushes for higher taxes but considers gaming the IRS acceptable. When it was disclosed that Sharpton had failed to file income taxes for several years, he quickly contacted his accountant and had him file for an extension. He then explained: "If you do not file intentionally, you're violating the law. If you notify them that you're filing late, you could not be intending to defraud. If I intended not to file, why would I instruct an accountant to inform them that I have not filed and that I intend to file?" That certainly clears things up. Regardless of where Sharpton actually stands with his accountant and the IRS, the confusion has not adversely affected his standing in liberal circles.

Former New York City mayor David Dinkins faced similar problems when it was revealed that he had failed to pay taxes (or even file a tax return) for five years. He used the same logic, in shorthand, to explain his situation. "I haven't committed a crime," he said. "What I did was fail to comply with the law."

Big bad corporations fail to pay their taxes, we often hear from the political left, and loopholes need to be closed. The accounting scandals at Enron are often portrayed as an example of excessive capitalism, perpetrated by free market conservatives who are greedily willing to cut corners to make a profit. But how do liberals and conservatives actually view the question of business ethics? Professors from San Jose State University and the University of North Carolina tried to find out. They asked business students at both schools: How serious a crime is tax evasion? The professors were surprised to discover that conservative students took the issue of accounting scandals and tax evasion very seriously. Liberal students considered it a less serious offense.[10]

When two professors surveyed 291 students on their attitudes toward cheating, they discovered that students who had a "liberal outlook," and who "reject the idea of absolute truth," were much more likely to find cheating acceptable than those who did not.[11]

These findings are not inconsistent with what we know about the ideas and beliefs that distinguish those on the left and the right. Modern liberalism offers a "flexible" view of truth, which means that those who embrace it are more prone to believe that cheating can be acceptable. Conservative values, on the other hand, translate into higher business ethics. Three professors conducted extensive surveys with 392 college students and reported their findings in the *Journal of Business Ethics*. They discovered that "stronger beliefs toward work ethic and conservatism" translates into "higher levels of ethical values." Several other studies found the same link.[12]

The political left often expresses real concern about corporate criminal behavior and exploitation, features that they say are inherent to a capitalist system. But on a personal level, liberals seem to have much less of a problem with outlaw capitalism than conservatives. Is it okay to buy goods that you know are stolen? According to the liberal prejudice, one would expect conservatives to have no moral qualms about this: Business is business. But in reality, liberals have less of a problem with this unethical behavior than conservatives. One-third of those who called themselves very liberal said it was okay to buy goods they knew were stolen, compared with only 17 percent of conservatives.[13] (Note to criminals: You probably have a better chance of selling those hot stereos in San Francisco than in Oklahoma City.)

Another academic study found similar results. Secular liberals were more likely than conservatives to say it was acceptable to engage in a variety of unethical behaviors. For example, they were more likely to say it is all right to drink a can of soda in a store without paying for it, and to avoid the truth when negotiating the price of a car.[14]

Bribery is one of those areas where you might expect universal agreement. Isn't everyone against public officials taking payoffs? And yet the World Values Survey finds that liberals are more willing to accept bribes than conservatives—by a sizable 10 percentage points.

This information confirms what you find in pretty much every survey: The farther you move to the right, the more of a problem people have with lying and cheating. When asked by the World Values Survey whether it is okay to avoid paying bus or subway fare, liberals—by a whopping 20 points—said they had no problem calling fare-jumping an acceptable practice.[15]

One survey by Democratic pollster Peter Hart found that liberal Democrats were much less concerned than conservatives about a potential Supreme Court nominee who had cheated in law school. Another found that liberals are almost two and a half times more likely to illegally download or trade music for free on the Internet.[16] I guess if you believe, like Marx, that property is theft, then stealing the fruits of a musician's labor is an act of political idealism.

Even when liberals find money that does not belong to them, they are much more likely to say it's okay to keep it. One study by two professors in the *Journal of Psychology* looked at 156 adults and found that "political liberalism" made a person more likely to justify "lying in your own interest," including "keeping money that you have found" instead of reporting it to the police.[17]

Liberals present themselves as other-directed, community-conscious good Samaritans. Yet the World Values Survey found that conservatives are 15 percent more likely to say that you must report damage you've done to a parked car than liberals.

Let's say you go to a restaurant and the waitress accidentally leaves items off the bill. Would you tell them about it? Your answer partly depends on your belief system. More than a third of liberals (34 percent) said they would cheat the restaurant out of the money, compared with just 18 percent of conservatives, according to the National Cultural Values Survey. Another study in the *Journal of Business Ethics* came up with the same result.[18]

What if a mistake happens at work or at school and someone else gets blamed for something you did or failed to do. Would you come forward and admit your mistake? Or would you cover up or deny it in order to protect yourself? Self-described progressives were more than twice as likely to select the second option when compared to conservatives (27 percent to 12 percent).[19]

Another study published in the *Journal of Business Ethics* found that secular relativists were much more willing to "let others take the blame" for their own ethical lapses. (Eighty-eight percent of conservatives said this was wrong; only 68 percent of liberals agreed.) The study also found that secular relativists were more accepting of "cheating on an exam," and were more willing to "copy a published article" and pass it off as their own.[20]

No one would claim that there aren't bad conservatives. It might also be objected that liberals are just more honest than conservatives, who may simply give the "right" answer in a survey because they know it is expected of them. But there is simply no evidence that this is the case. As was pointed out earlier, repeated studies have shown that one's ideology does not appear to influence one's candor on a survey. On the other hand, the beliefs and values we hold to be true tend to affect our behavior in material ways. Even if they are more honored in the breach than the observance, as the saying goes, the fact that they have moral authority in our eyes will have a salutary effect.

The same must be said of their opposites. Cheating and dishonesty are the sort of behaviors that if you are comfortable with them in one part of your life, they will show up in others. A study of four hundred business executives found that those who cheated on their golf scores were also much more likely to cheat in business.[21] When news reports surfaced that Bill Clinton was prone to cheating on his golf scores (Tiger Woods called it "interesting math" when he played a round with the former president), no one seemed particularly surprised. The same seems to apply when we look at nonfinancial cheating and dishonesty.[22]

In America today there exists what might be called a philandering gap. Both liberals and conservatives have been unfaithful to their spouses; lust is not a partisan political passion. And yet, there is a yawning gap in attitudes between liberals and conservatives as to whether cheating is *acceptable*. Thousands of Americans were asked by the General Social Survey: Is it okay to cheat on your spouse? As one might expect, 86 percent of those who described themselves as very conservative said flat-out "No." But only 59 percent of those who described themselves as very liberal agreed with them. Those who called themselves "liberal" or "slightly liberal" did only marginally better—63 and 68 percent respectively.[23]

The National Cultural Values Survey found similar results. More than a third (35 percent) of self-described "progressives" said "there are some situations where adultery is understandable." Only 3 percent of conservatives agreed. Fully 95 percent of conservatives said "adultery is always wrong." Only 61 percent of "progressives" agreed. (Moms and dads: The next time your daughter comes home from college and says she met the man of her dreams at the campus socialist club—be very concerned.)

Many liberals seem to adopt a *Desperate Housewives* attitude toward infidelity. "It's just sex," said one of the characters in the show. "It's totally harmless."[24]

On any question of honesty asked, those on the liberal-left have a much more "flexible" definition than conservatives. They find it much easier to justify lying for a financial advantage or, shall we say, some affection on the side. As I said earlier, no one has a corner on honesty and truth. But this evidence conforms with the realities of what we saw in chapter 1: Modern liberals are more self-oriented and less guided than conservatives by external standards and values.

Beginning in the 1960s, liberalism embraced the notion that lying was not necessarily a bad thing. Many of today's political leaders were brought up in this atmosphere. Saul Alinsky was a left-wing organizer who influenced literally thousands of people on the left during his lifetime. Among them was Hillary Clinton, who wrote her senior thesis at Wellesley on his approach to politics. Sen. Barack Obama also claims to be indebted to Alinsky, using many of his techniques as a community organizer in Chicago during the 1980s.[25]

Alinsky was a radical who had little patience for abstract concepts like truth and ethics. One of his political rules: "Ethical standards must be elastic to stretch with the times."[26] He encouraged people to be relativists because it gave them greater ethical wiggle room. The effective political advocate, according to Alinsky, "does not have a fixed truth—truth to him is relative and changing, everything to him is relative and changing. He is a political relativist." One shouldn't get too caught up in worrying about ethical lapses. "It is a world not of angels but of angles, where men speak of moral principles but act on power principles; a world where we are always moral and our enemies always immoral." Everyone is corrupt and dishonest, according to Alinsky. "Life is a corrupting process from the time a child learns to play his mother off against his father in the politics of when to go to bed; he who fears corruption fears life." Worrying about honesty is a waste of time, he argues. "The means-and-ends moralists or non-doers always wind up on their ends without any means."[27]

In her autobiography, Hillary Clinton professes that she has but one "fundamental disagreement" with Alinsky. "He believed you could change the system only from the outside. I didn't."[28]

Conservatives have been caught telling whoppers from time to time, and usually pay a political price for it. But many liberals seem less concerned with the pursuit of truth because they really don't think it exists. Many on the left embrace Nietzsche's famous dictum: "There are no facts, only interpretations." Bill Clinton must have had this in mind when he uttered the words: "It depends on what the meaning of 'is' is. . . ." This means that on the national stage, liberals enjoy a wider moral latitude. Conservative political figures are held to a higher standard because conservative voters care more about honesty. Liberal leaders who are dishonest rarely if ever get punished by liberal voters because they are more willing to make excuses for dishonesty.

Consider a few examples. When Wisconsin state senator and majority leader Mary Panzer (R) decided to run for governor, she noted on her résumé that she had graduated from the University of Wisconsin at Madison when in fact she had not. She was handily defeated in the Republican primary. When Elaine Musselman ran for Congress as a Republican in Kentucky, it was revealed that she had neither of the two degrees that she claimed on her résumé. Her support quickly evaporated and she dropped out of the race.

When State Representative Royall Switzler ran for the Republican nomination for governor of Massachusetts in 1986, he falsely claimed that he had been a Green Beret in Vietnam. What happened? He withdrew from the race in embarrassment. Congressman Bruce Caputo, a candidate for lieutenant governor in New York, was driven out of politics when it was revealed that he hadn't served in Vietnam or graduated with honors from Harvard Business School as he claimed.[29]

Many on the liberal-left don't suffer setbacks to their careers when caught doing the same thing. Sen. Joe Biden claimed he received academic distinction in college, received a full scholarship for law school, won an international moot-court competition, and finished in the top half of his law school class. None of this was true—but it didn't seem to cost him any political support. He wins by large margins and now runs as a presidential candidate. Indeed, he is considered one of the most serious and ethically scrupulous Democrats in Washington. Fellow senator Tom Harkin claimed that he'd flown airplanes in Vietnam. "I was flying F-4s and F-8s on combat air patrols and photoreconnaissance support missions," he told a group of veterans. This was completely false—he had never been to Vietnam. And yet he didn't face any political repercussions from his base of supporters. Neither did Atlantic City mayor Bob Levy, who falsely claimed that he was a Green Beret in Vietnam. Democrats continued to rally behind him anyway.[30]

When it was revealed that Larry Lawrence, wealthy entrepreneur, funder of liberal causes, and friend of Bill Clinton, had manufactured a heroic war record so he could be buried at Arlington National Cemetery, he was actually defended by some on the left. Donald Kaul, Washington columnist for the *Des Moines Register*, actually suggested that by lying, Lawrence had proven himself to be morally superior to the likes of Rush Limbaugh, Newt Gingrich, and Pat Buchanan, who also never served in the military. With his fabrication, said Kaul, Lawrence showed that he had at least *wanted* to be a hero.[31]

Former San Francisco mayor Willie Brown captured the attitude prevalent among many modern liberals when one of his close aides was caught falsely claiming on a résumé that he had gone to college. "I don't know anyone who doesn't lie on his résumé," he said.[32] Alcee Hastings was a federal judge who was indicted and impeached by the U.S. Congress for apparently soliciting a bribe during a federal criminal probe. And yet he was elected to Congress and enjoyed the esteem of many of his colleagues as he climbed in seniority on Capitol Hill. Were Hastings a conservative Republican, it is highly unlikely that he would ever have been elected to office.

Sex scandals deal different results depending on whether you are a conservative or a liberal. In 1983 a sex scandal involving congressional pages erupted in Washington. The fate of those involved depended on their politics. Congressman Dan Crane, a popular three-term representative from Illinois, was defeated for reelection in 1984 after it was disclosed that he had a consensual relationship with a seventeen-year-old female page while a member of Congress. Congressman Gerry Studds, a liberal from Massachusetts, was implicated in the same scandal for doing exactly the same thing; the only difference being that Studds was involved with a seventeen-year-old male page. But whereas Crane tearfully apologized for what he had done, Studds did not. Indeed, Studds was defiant on the House floor. And while Crane was rejected for reelection by his conservative Republican district, Studds continued to win reelection in his liberal Massachusetts district until his retirement in 1997. Conservative Republicans often get in trouble because their base of supporters is less tolerant of lying.

When Congressman Mark Foley of Florida was implicated in sending troubling instant messages to male pages in 2006, he resigned quickly under pressure from colleagues and supporters in his district. Sen. Larry Craig was similarly disgraced for his conduct in a men's bathroom at the Minneapolis airport. One can only wonder: Were either one a liberal Democrat from San Francisco or Massachusetts, would they have been forced to resign?

The answer is no, because many modern liberals have a very tolerant attitude toward sexual indiscretions of all kinds. This became apparent during the Clinton-Lewinsky scandal. President Clinton lied to a federal grand jury and he did it in fine fashion, denying that he had a sexual relationship with Monica Lewinsky. This was based on the notion that Lewinsky might have had sex with him, but he did not have sex with her. "If the deponent is a person who has sex performed on him, then the contact . . . is with the lips of another person," which doesn't constitute sex, he explained.

After the scandal became public, Clinton explained his remorse for "lying to my family, my staff, and most of all the American people." Then he offered what he called "not an excuse but a partial explanation" for why he had lied in the first place. "In November of 1995 I was involved in a titanic struggle with the Republican Congress. They were trying to change the nature of government in our life, take the country in a different direction. A direction some of you might have agreed with, but I didn't and I didn't want to be President if that was where my country was going. So I was determined to stop it. So they shut government down and only a few people were legally permitted to come to work in the White House. The whole place was being run by the young volunteers [including Monica]. And that's what I meant when I said, 'because I could.' "

When he appeared later on *Oprah*, he went a step further and argued that he had not lied to protect himself but to protect the country. If the truth had come out, he told her, it would "cause me to be run from office and that the bad guys would win." In short, he lied to serve the national interest.[33]

A survey taken after the Lewinsky scandal and the scandal over pardons in the final days of his administration found that 41 percent of liberals considered Clinton to be an honest person. Honesty, after all, is a relative term. And many rallied to his defense, arguing that adultery was not necessarily a bad thing; indeed, it might even be a good thing. Congressman Dick Gephardt upbraided those who criticized Clinton by saying they were after "unattainable goals of morality." Unattainable? Honesty and fidelity? Marshall Herskovitz, creator of such Hollywood staples as *thirtysomething*, explained: "Clinton is a set of contradictions, and many of those contradictions work quite well within the moral structure of Hollywood."

Far from being something bad, novelist Jane Smiley saw Clinton's conduct as confirming his trustworthiness. "Maybe what Clinton did in the Oval Office was love, or infatuation, or just sex," she wrote in the *New Yorker*. "At the very least, it was a desire to make a connection with another person, a habitual desire for which Clinton is well known. . . . this desire is something I trust."[34]

Dr. Sam Sahehan, a physician who deals with these matters in Marina Del Ray, California, likewise argued that Clinton's infidelity was a good thing. "It's moral realism," he told the media. "People see the president under a lot of stress and it may be necessary for an additional outlet, and if that outlet is with a beautiful young woman who helps him be happy, why bother him? Realizing the president is only a human being like themselves, most Americans understand his urge to be with other women and condone it."[35]

Even after Clinton's various ethical problems became public, 83 percent of those who described themselves as "extremely liberal" agreed that "moral" was a good word to describe Bill Clinton.[36] This lack of liberal concern about honesty and fidelity was not lost on the mobster John Gotti, who saw a clear double standard at work. Gotti was caught on a federal wiretap saying, "If he [Clinton] had an Italian last name they would've electrocuted him."[37]

Now contrast Clinton's performance with that of conservative Republicans caught in similar predicaments. Several of them, such as Congressman Bob Livingston of Louisiana, were forced to resign. Liberals were selectively outraged by Livingston's conduct. In no case were there conservatives defending the actions or calling them a necessary stress-reduction technique.

Former vice president Gore has numerous times over the course of his career told lies, some minor, some real whoppers. He has claimed that he created the Strategic Petroleum Reserve (it actually started two years before he was in Congress), had been sung a particular union song as a lullaby (it was written when he was a wee lad of twenty-seven), and that his mother paid more for her arthritis medicine than she did for her dog's arthritis pills. (The statistic actually came from a government report.) Stretching the truth happens often in politics, but Gore has stretched it for political gain regarding tragic family circumstances.

At the Democratic National Convention in 1996, Al Gore gave a heart-wrenching description of his sister Nancy's death from cancer. The vice president explained how Nancy started smoking at thirteen and three years later had a lung removed. "Her husband," Gore explained, "and all of us who loved her so much tried to get her to stop smoking. Of course she should have. But she couldn't." As she was stricken with cancer, her family took turns sitting by her hospital bed. "By then her pain was nearly unbearable, and as a result they used very powerful painkillers. Eventually, it got so bad they had to use such heavy doses that she could barely retain consciousness. . . . She looked up and from out of that haze, her eyes focused tensely on me. She couldn't speak, but I felt clearly I knew she was forming a question: Do you bring me hope? But all I could do was to say back to her, with all the gentleness in my heart, 'I love you.' And then I knelt by her bed and held her hand. And in a very short time her breathing became labored and then she breathed her last breath." Gore then said he made a vow: "Tomorrow morning, another thirteen-year-old girl will start smoking. I love her, too. Three thousand young people in America will start smoking tomorrow. One thousand of them will die a death not unlike my sister's, and that is why, until I draw my last breath, I will pour my heart and soul into the cause of protecting our children from the dangers of smoking."

The story seemed inspiring enough. Gore's sister had indeed died of smoking-induced cancer in 1984. But it turned out that when he campaigned for president four years later, he had extolled the virtues of tobacco farming. Stumping for votes in North Carolina, he had told tobacco farmers, "Throughout most of my life, I raised tobacco. I want you to know that with my own hands, all of my life, I put it in the plant beds and transferred it. I've hoed it. I've chopped it. I've shredded it, spiked it, put it in the barn and stripped it and sold it." Gore drawled out the word "tobacco" so it became *tobakka* to emphasize how much he loved the stuff. And Gore family records revealed that he continued to grow tobacco or lease his land to grow tobacco until at least 1991, a full seven years after his emotional pledge to thwart tobacco consumption in memory of his dying sister.[38]

So Gore was using his sister's death to denounce smoking and the tobacco industry, knowing that he had grown tobacco, courted the tobacco industry, and defended growing tobacco many years after she died. Gore was pressed by reporters for an explanation. "I felt a numbness [from her death] that prevented me from integrating into all aspects of my life the implications of what the tragedy really meant," he offered in an unapologetic apology. "We are in the midst of a profound shift in the way we approach issues. I really do believe that in our politics and personal lives, we are seeing an effort to integrate our emotional lives in a more balanced fashion."

When asked about his lying on several other issues, Gore explained that these were not actually lies, but were instead "rhetorical excesses and leaps of faith." This sounds a lot like director Oliver Stone, when he was confronted by journalists questioning many of the "facts" and "truths" that he professed to offer in his film *JFK*. Alleging that he had proof that President Kennedy was killed by a conspiracy involving LBJ, the Mafia, the CIA, and the Pentagon, reporters challenged him on numerous factual points. Stone's defense? There really is no such thing as truth. "I have come to have severe doubts about Columbus, Washington, the Civil War being fought for slavery, the Indian Wars, World War I, World War II, the supposed fight against Nazism and/or Japanese control of resources in Southeast Asia. I've doubted everything. I don't even know if I was born and who my parents were. It may be virtual reality." He went on to explain, "Even if I am totally wrong . . . I am still right."[39]

When former Clinton labor secretary and prominent liberal Robert Reich released his memoir *Locked in the Cabinet,* he included in it tales of conflict and high drama with conservative Republican senators and congressmen. There were all sorts of contentious hearings where Sir Robert slayed the conservative dragons in verbal combat over benefits for workers. Then Jonathan Rauch, an intrepid Washington writer, compared Reich's account with the actual transcripts of the meetings that were available to the public. The meetings Reich called "raucous and confrontational" were actually calm and businesslike. Much of the dialogue Reich reported never really happened. Reich's explanation? "I was absolutely true to my memory," he said. He also updated the introduction to the book and added the phrase: "Memory is fallible."

For many on the liberal-left, lying is not just a matter of bolstering a résumé or enhancing past events for present gain. True to the memory of Saul Alinsky, some actually embrace it as a form of political action and a virtuous act. They call it "lying for justice."

Activist Mitch Snyder became famous in the 1980s for his vigorous attacks on the Reagan administration and what he considered its lack of concern for the plight of the homeless. He became a darling of the media for his strong language and his detailed claims that there were literally millions of homeless Americans wandering the streets. When he stated categorically that there were between 2 and 3 million homeless Americans, it became accepted as fact and was widely reported. But when he was asked by Ted Koppel on *Nightline* how he had arrived at that figure, he admitted that he basically made it up. "Everybody demanded it, everybody said we want a number. . . . We got on the phone, made lots of calls, we talked to lots of people, and we said, 'Okay, here are some numbers.' They have no meaning, no value." After those words left Snyder's mouth, no one seemed to bat an eye. Koppel didn't challenge him on his lying, and no one on the left denounced him. After all, he had done it in the name of social justice.[40]

Fifteen years later, the hot issue in Washington, D.C., was partial birth abortion, and Ron Fitzsimmons, executive director of the National Coalition of Abortion Providers, was called to testify about the procedure. Fitzsimmons sat in front of a congressional committee and explained that the procedure should not be outlawed because it was extremely rare and hardly ever used. A few years later he admitted to the media that he had "lied through my teeth" in making that statement. It was hardly a "rare" procedure. But Fitzsimmons's politically useful lie didn't cause a peep of protest. Indeed, many feminist groups regard him as a hero.

When Tawana Brawley charged that she had been abducted and sexually assaulted by a gang of white men, people were understandably outraged. But when it was revealed that she had made the whole incident up, that didn't give *The Nation* magazine pause. "In cultural perspective, if not in fact, it doesn't matter whether the crime occurred or not," they explained. It still made a valid point about race in America.[41]

In the early 1970s, CBS News reporter Charles Kuralt did a story about poverty in the American South and actually showed footage of a baby dying on national television. It caused quite a stir and became a national sensation. "The baby is dying of starvation," Kuralt said. "He was an American. Now he is dead." It made for dramatic footage. But the fact was, the baby didn't die of starvation; it was a three-month-old premature baby, born to a mother severely injured in an automobile accident. The parents were not poor, and the child had received all the medical care available. The story, as presented, was based on a series of falsehoods. But CBS News executive Richard Salant defended the lie, saying that the "essential truths of the story" were still there.[42]

The same defense was offered in 2004 by *60 Minutes* correspondent Dan Rather, who had aired a politically damaging story about George W. Bush's supposed pattern of absence from the Texas Air National Guard during the Vietnam War, based on a memo that turned out to be a forgery. Rather refused to retract the story, famously claiming that the memo was "fake but accurate."

It's bad enough that liberal politicians get a pass from their constituents for their lies and bad behavior. But modern liberalism's lack of interest in truth and honesty extends beyond politics to the hallowed halls of academe. Academics can be particularly adept at lying and making excuses for it. As anthropologist F. G. Bailey notes in the book *The Prevalence of Deceit*, "The academic arena is populated by deceivers." What makes them particularly troublesome is that they "practice deceit while being enthusiasts for truth."[43]

Liberals in the world of academe have embraced the notion that there is no real truth. Richard Rorty, one of the leading exponents of pragmatism in American philosophy, held that there is no such thing as truth. All that exists is opinion. Professor Thomas Bender of New York University calls scholars who insist on accuracy "fact fetishists."[44] Two academics from the University of Pennsylvania explained in one professional journal, "We are all engaged in writing a kind of propaganda. . . . Rather than believe in the absolute truth of what we are writing, we must believe in the moral or political position we are taking with it."[45]

When it was discovered that California poet laureate and University of California at San Diego professor Quincy Troupe had lied about receiving college degrees, the university didn't plan to fire him. They only accepted his resignation because of public outcry.

When it was revealed that Edward Said, a radical professor at Columbia University, made up the fact that he had spent the first twelve years of his life in Jerusalem (actually he was living very comfortably in Cairo) to heighten his claims to the mantle of the Palestinian cause, Said's colleagues vigorously defended him. Said didn't really lie, one of them explained. What he did was "compress all his unique gifts in the form of a personal narrative as living testimony of the essence of his Palestinianhood." Can you imagine trying that one in the real world? You didn't lie on your résumé, you "compressed your unique gifts into the form of a personal narrative."

When Yale professor Paul de Man died in 1983, he was hailed by many on the left as one of the most courageous thinkers of the twentieth century. One of the champions of the "deconstructionist" approach to literary criticism, "De Man came to represent all those in the Modern Language Association [MLA] who had championed modernist literature," it was said by his colleagues.[46] One colleague claimed, "In a profession full of fakeness, he was for real."[47] Four years later it was disclosed that de Man had written more than two hundred articles for a pro-Nazi newspaper during the Second World War, engaged in shady business practices, and then fled Europe, abandoning his wife and three children. He moved to the United States, remarried without divorcing his first wife, and created a new personal history. He claimed at various times to have been a translator in London during the war, and even to have been a resistance fighter in France. When news came out after his death that he had completely lied about his past, many of his colleagues didn't seem to have a problem with it. Jacques Derrida, the founder of deconstruction, offered a defense that was accepted by too many of his colleagues: There is what happened and what de

Man thought had happened, and both are equally legitimate. (Try that the next time your boss asks you to explain your overbudget expense report.)[48]

One of the most popular books on college campuses is the autobiography of Rigoberta Menchu, now an icon of the international left. Menchu's book is a moving account of growing up poor and exploited in rural Guatemala and how she became a peasant activist. Largely because of this book, she was awarded the Nobel Peace Prize in 1992. Her autobiography has been assigned in hundreds of classrooms around the country and held up as a noble example of how to fight imperialism, colonialism, sexism, and capitalism. But when writer David Stoll began looking at her life story, he quickly discovered that she had made up key elements of her life. The claim that a brother died of malnutrition was a lie—he lived a quite prosperous life. She was not illiterate, as she claimed, but the product of a prestigious Catholic boarding school. None of this seemed to bother her liberal fans or the professors who pushed her book. Her book was "true in spirit, if not in fact, and therefore honest," one academic explained. One faculty member became upset at a student who mentioned Stoll's reporting because—imagine it—"It tended to discredit her." The chair of Wellesley's Spanish Department told one reporter, "Whether her book is true or not, I don't care." (So much for speaking "truth" to power!) Her book continues to be required reading on college campuses across America. In such an atmosphere, it should come as no surprise that many liberal academics are prepared to defend lying when it serves their ideological purposes. Meanwhile, many of them are no doubt attending "Bush Lied!" rallies.

Sometimes lying and cheating is defended on the left even when the consequences are plain and real. When the liberal Miami-Dade School Board discovered that dozens of teachers had bought transcripts and grades for continuing education courses they were required to take but never did, they actually anguished about whether or not to fire the teachers. Board member Evelyn Greer was concerned that it would cause "disruptions." "It baffles me, just baffles me, to have disruptions at the class level," she explained. It was only by the narrowest of votes—five to four—that the cheating teachers were let go.

Likewise, when school officials in New York City were caught helping students cheat so they could pass a mandatory state test, the New York City school chancellor, Rudy Crew, in effect came to their defense, arguing that the tests had made them do it. "Any time you have this kind of mounting pressure about holding children to a standard, it shouldn't come as any wonder that there are going to be people who will find a creative way of cheating."[49] The consequences of such cheating, as it affects the quality of education, was apparently not part of the calculus.

When a cheating scandal erupted on the Duke University campus (students were getting together to answer take-home exams), the attitude of many was that it was no big deal. *Business Week* called it "postmodern learning," and Professor Robert Sutton saw the cheating as a sign of initiative. "If you found somebody to help you write an exam, in our view that's a sign of an inventive person who gets stuff done."[50]

Yale law professor Stephen Carter, in his book *Integrity*, argues that integrity requires three things, the first and most important being an ability to discern what is right and wrong. But modern liberalism has become so hypnotized by moral relativism that it is hard for its adherents to make such judgments. They are willing to excuse all kinds of dishonest behavior, or argue that no excuse is necessary at all. Because if there is no law, then everything is permitted.

So if your uncle Bob from San Francisco offers to sell you his Prius, you just might want to take it to the shop and check out the transmission.

5.

ANGER MANAGEMENT
How Modern Liberalism Promotes Anger

When Hillary Clinton gets angry, report the *Chicago Sun-Times* and *Baltimore Sun,* she apparently has a habit of throwing things. During her tenure as first lady, it was reported that she threw a lamp at her husband. On another occasion, a prominent senator told the magazine that he "overheard Hillary shouting at Bill and threatening to throw something at him."[1] Hillary Clinton denies all this. As she told Barbara Walters, "I mean, you know, I have a pretty good arm. If I'd thrown a lamp at somebody, I think you would have known about it."

But if Senator Clinton does have a proclivity to launch projectiles, she is not alone. Liberals in general are much more likely to throw things when they get angry when compared to conservatives. According to the authoritative General Social Survey, those who consider themselves "very liberal" are *three times* more likely to "let fly" when compared with corresponding conservatives. (Unfortunately, the data offers no insight into target selection or rate of accuracy.)[2]

To hear it from the popular media, you might tend to believe that conservatives are seething and angry, responsible for all the venom and rage in our country today. It started back in 1994 when conservatives took back the Congress. Then ABC News anchor Peter Jennings, attempting to explain the Democrats' otherwise inexplicable loss of power, claimed that it was not the result of a rational choice, but anger. He went on to compare conservative voters to two-year-olds. "Ask parents of any two-year-old and they can tell you about those temper tantrums: the stomping feet, the rolling eyes, the screaming. It's clear that the anger controls the child and not the other way around. . . . the voters had a temper tantrum last week."[3]

Steven Roberts of *U.S. News & World Report* likewise explained that anger and bitterness were behind the victory. "They are not voting Republican tonight," he sagely pronounced. "They are voting against a lot of unhappiness in their lives."

The image of angry conservatives picked up steam as talk radio exploded in popularity. Surely it was not possible that the booming interest in talk radio had to do with the opportunity to talk about public issues outside the control of the dominant liberal media. Instead it was an exercise in venting pent-up anger. Evan Thomas of *Newsweek* complained about "this constant anger" on talk radio that "attaches itself to different issues."

Conservatives were called at various times "snarling," "fuming," and "deeply angry" by the mainstream media. When the Murraugh Federal Building was bombed in Oklahoma City, the media was quick to affix blame to conservatives. Arguing that conservative ideas had provoked violence, Carl Rowan of the *Washington Post* explained: "I am absolutely certain the harsher rhetoric of the Gingriches and the Doles creates a climate of violence in America." *Time* magazine's Richard Lacayo wrote that "the inflamed rhetoric is suddenly an unindicted co-conspirator in the blast." Bryant Gumbel, then cohosting the *Today* show, said that the blast occurred because of the anger "coming from the right and those who cater to angry white men."[4] President Clinton boldly claimed (without any evidence) that conservative talk show hosts "leave the impression—by their very words—that violence is acceptable."

Suddenly there emerged what the media called "the angry white male." No, they were not talking about Al Franken or Ward Churchill. Instead they had in mind the ordinary conservatives once praised for helping to make America what it is. Now they were suddenly dangerous. *Newsweek* ran a cover story titled "White Male Paranoia." Conservatives were insecure, angry, and controlling, the article explained. They were also prone to violence. *Newsweek* quoted a woman who called conservative voters "a bunch of shallow, bald, middle-aged men with character disorders. They don't have the emotional capacity that it takes to qualify as human beings. The one good thing about these white, male, almost-extinct mammals is that they're growing old. We get to watch them die." (Apparently bitterness and anger and a wish to see your adversaries die are perfectly acceptable—in liberals.)[5]

Hollywood even made a timely movie about the misadventures of an angry white male. *Falling Down*, starring Michael Douglas, offered the following tagline: "The adventures of an ordinary man at war with the everyday world." The film showed Douglas, a laid-off defense industry worker, driving around L.A. (in a car with the vanity license plate "D-FENCE") getting angry at everyone—gays, blacks, women, even workers at a fast-food restaurant. Naturally, like any conservative, he settles his nerves by using automatic weapons.

The notion that conservatives are angry, easily provoked, and capable of brutal acts of violence has become accepted wisdom for many today. Bill Maher says that "Republicans need anger management" because of the "vein-popping, gut-churning rage that consumes the entire right wing." Sen. Tom Daschle, then majority leader in the Senate, complained about the "shrill rhetoric" of conservatives and warned darkly that "shrill power motivates," presumably to violence. The ever-balanced and judicious liberal blogger James Wolcott considers the conservative personality profile to be similar to that of a mass murderer. In his estimation, Dennis Rader, the infamous BTK serial killer from Wichita, Kansas, is "the nightmare embodiment of the Red State personality."

Even levelheaded analysts like Tom Edsall, formerly of the *Washington Post,* have accepted the myth that conservatives are inherently angry. "Liberals," he explains in the *New Republic,* "by their very nature don't get as angry as conservatives do." I guess he hasn't talked politics recently with Al Franken.

Jonathan Klein, president of CNN, claims that conservative anger is the real reason behind the success of cable rival Fox News. "A 'progressive' or 'liberal' network probably couldn't reach the same sort of an audience, because liberals tend to like to sample a lot of opinions," he claimed without offering a shred of evidence. "They pride themselves on that. And you know, they don't get too worked up about anything. And they're pretty morally relativistic. And so, you know, they allow for a lot of that stuff. You know, Fox is very appealing to people who like to get worked up over things."[6]

Right, Mr. Klein—liberals like Air America's Randi Rhodes and Daily Kos founder Markos Moulitsas don't like to get "worked up" over little things like the "stolen" 2000 election or the war in Iraq. They welcome conservative views and always treat their adversaries civilly and with an open mind. Is that a description of any reality you recognize?

Academics have also pushed the idea that conservatives are prone to get "worked up," often with dangerous consequences. Typical of the "scholarly" approach is the book *Social Rage* by Bonnie Berry, which claims that conservatives are much more likely to erupt in "rage," citing the example of fringe militia groups. Meanwhile, when those on the left get angry, she explains, it is justified.[7] The academic journal *Social Policy* likewise made the case that "conservatives are driven by rage," as opposed to liberals who are motivated by reason.[8]

But the idea that conservatives are an angry lot while liberals are calm and rational is, quite simply, a myth. Indeed, the opposite is true. As we shall see, the farther to the left you go, the more anger you encounter. Liberals are not only angrier about politics than conservatives, they also tend to be angrier in their daily lives. They are more likely to seek revenge against those who anger them, more likely to hold a grudge, and more likely to take offense at criticism.

Visit a college campus today and the anger and violence is almost exclusively on the left. In recent years conservative speakers have been physically attacked with ice cream pies (Bill Kristol), salad dressing (Pat Buchanan), custard cream pie (Ann Coulter), and a shoe (Richard Perle). I have yet to find a case where Michael Moore or Stephen Colbert have been greeted by students wielding deadly dairy products.

Much of the anger these days is of course directed at President George W. Bush. After the 2004 election, the editor of the *Boston Phoenix,* a widely read alternative publication, wrote an angry screed titled: "Screw You America: Sometimes Fish in the Barrel Deserve to Die." The article began: "Don't forgive my anger." Jonathan Chait in the normally levelheaded *New Republic* likewise wrote a much-discussed article titled: "The Case for Bush Hatred." He began: "I hate President George W. Bush. There, I said it."

Novelist Jane Smiley explained that same year: "I woke up early this morning and lay awake anxious and angry about political matters. I see people who are Republicans as people who have aligned themselves with the worst features of the American character. . . . I actually don't mind being angry. I don't think liberals mind. I think it's a good thing."[9]

During the 2004 campaign there were stylish "Kill Bush" T-shirts and messenger bags available for purchase (strangely, no one produced a line of "Kill Kerry" products).[10] The left also launched a series of campaigns on college campuses to motivate their voters. *The Nation* magazine called it "the angry mosh" vote.[11] Author Peter Wood in his thoughtful book *A Bee in the Mouth: Anger in America* notes that the left has embraced "anger chic." It is now stylish to be angry.

Assassination literature has become popular even in mainstream circles. Avant-garde author Nicholson Baker wrote a novel titled *Checkpoint* about two old friends, Jay and Ben, who discuss how best to murder President Bush. Published by Alfred A. Knopf, the book includes discussions of various lethal weapons that might be employed to do the trick. *Booklist* praised it as "a work of provocative and razor-sharp fiction." (The *New York Times Book Review* had the sense to call it a "scummy little book.") But as Baker explained in a *Washington Post* interview, his motive was hardly artistic. Bush's actions "make me so angry," he said. "And it's a new kind of anger."

Not to be outdone, *New York Times* bestselling author Sarah Vowell wrote *Assassination Vacation,* about assassinated presidents—Lincoln, Garfield, and McKinley. She is so angry at Bush that she can envision his assassination. As she told one newspaper: "If I can summon this much bitterness toward a presidential human being, I can sort of, kind of see how this amount of bile or more, teaming up with disappointment, unemployment, delusions of grandeur and mental illness, could prompt a crazier narcissistic creep to buy one of this country's widely available handguns. Not that I, I repeat, condone that." Her major concern if Bush were assassinated? "I don't think I can stomach watching that man get turned into a martyr if he were killed."[12]

When conservatives expressed concern about Bush hatred going too far, influential liberals like *New York Times* columnist Paul Krugman would have none of it. "All this fuss about civility," he wrote, "is an attempt to bully critics into unilaterally disarming—into being demure and respectful of the president." A liberal campus activist agreed, complaining that it was not possible to do politics without anger. "We play politics like a game of checkers, bemoaning the loss of civility, or whatever . . . as if politics is something that should be played without passion, without anger."[13]

This sort of political anger is not limited to cranks or novelists. Even some calm and rational liberals have succumbed. Northwestern University professor Gary Alan Fine tells of a meeting among academics in Washington, D.C., where a "distinguished social scientist" proclaimed her "hatred" of George W. Bush. When someone said it was his politics she hated, she corrected them and explained, no, she "hated him." "She felt nauseated and angry when she watched him. She was not just intellectually offended but morally so."[14]

Some conservatives have termed this phenomenon "Bush derangement syndrome," on the theory (plausible enough) that the president's unwelcome electoral victories and actions in the war on terror have thrown the left into an angry frenzy. But this misses the larger point: People on the liberal-left are angry to begin with. Bush has simply become the object of their anger.

In general, liberals tend to be an agitated sort. And the more liberal they are, the more likely they are to say that they are agitated. When asked by the General Social Survey if they had felt peaceful in the last month, 77 percent of conservatives said all or most of the time, compared with 53 percent of those who called themselves very liberal.[15] That's a considerable gap.

The survey also found that liberals are angry more often than conservatives, and their anger is more intense. Liberals were almost twice as likely to have been angry at someone in the last five days—27 percent versus 14 percent of conservatives (10 percent said they were angry with someone *every day* in the last week!). What's more, that anger isn't focused, but global, projected in all directions. Those on the left were more likely to get angry at work. But they were almost twice as likely to say they had been angry at a perfect stranger in the past week. And when liberals get angry, they get very angry. Asked to rate their fury on a scale of 1 to 10, 22 percent placed their anger at 10 ("most intense") compared with just 15 percent of conservatives.[16]

As pointed out earlier, those on the left are much more likely to throw things when they get angry. (Perhaps one should hide the cutlery when discussing politics with lefty relatives.) But they are also much more likely to seek help from the pharmacy or liquor cabinet. Those who described themselves as very liberal were *five times* more likely to say that they "had a drink or took a pill" to deal with their anger. Thirty percent said this was how they coped.[17]

Liberals are almost twice as likely as conservatives to have used profanity in public during the past month—fully half of self-described liberals, compared with just 27 percent of conservatives.[18] As Michael Lind has pointed out (in *The Nation* magazine no less), "The left treats the normalization of profanity and obscenity as though it were somehow progressive."[19]

Liberals also seem to hunger for revenge in disproportionate numbers. The General Social Survey found that those who described themselves as "very liberal" were twice as likely to fantasize about revenging themselves on the person they were angry with and *three times* more likely (17 percent to 6 percent) to have actually *done something* to get back at someone who had hurt or offended them in the past month. Another survey found similar results.[20]

Liberal icons cater to this anger. I don't simply mean biting commentary, which is common among all political pundits. I mean real anger, which they often display proudly as a sign of authenticity. Al Franken, the liberal pundit and failed talk show host turned would-be politician, has been extremely successful by spewing anger at his opponents. And he's not afraid to become physically aggressive when it suits his purposes. When he showed up at the *Michael Medved Show* for a brief interview, he got angry with the producer and reportedly threw a chair. On the *Laura Ingraham Show,* Franken got into a shouting match with the show's producer and called him "an asshole." A scuffle ensued and security was eventually called. (Security also had to be called when he visited the Fox News Channel.) When a heckler appeared at a Howard Dean rally during the 2004 presidential primary, Franken tackled the man and threw him to the ground. "I got down low and took his legs out," he bragged.

When Franken released his book *The Truth with Lies,* he put together a small promotional skit for Amazon.com in which he kneed a self-described "right-wing jerk" in the groin. As the victim kneels over in pain, Franken hits him with a stool, sending him to the ground. One of his fans then finishes the man off with a bottle. Sure, conservative icons can get angry—but it's hard to imagine Sean Hannity would ever suggest that he favors beating up liberals.

Mere proximity to conservatives is enough to make some

liberals angry. When Franken ran into John O'Neill, who headed up Swiftboat Veterans for Truth, Franken said that just being near him was enough to make him angry. Singer Linda Ronstadt, an outspoken liberal, explained that she doesn't want to know if conservatives are in her midst. "It's a real conflict for me when I go to a concert and find out somebody in the audience is a Republican or a fundamentalist Christian. It can cloud my enjoyment. I'd rather not know."[21] (Can you imagine Dennis Miller getting angry because someone who bought a ticket to his show disagrees with him?)

New Republic writer Jonathan Chait explains that the mere existence of Bush causes psychological problems for his family. His sister-in-law "describes Bush's existence as an oppressive force, a constant weight on her shoulder, just knowing that George Bush is president."[22]

Michael Moore is also prone to fits of rage. He famously threw a temper tantrum at a London playhouse when he claimed he was not being paid enough. The bar staff, which was being paid about eight dollars an hour, was not spared. "He stormed around all day screaming at everybody, even the five-pound-an-hour bar staff, telling us how we were all con men and useless. Then he went onstage and did it in public." The staff eventually rebelled and Moore was forced to apologize.

In almost all of his significant working relationships, Moore has been prone to angry battles. He left as editor of the magazine *Mother Jones* after a series of angry arguments, and quit as the editor of a newsletter for Ralph Nader, again because of angry disagreements. His feuds with film producers Bob and Harvey Weinstein are legendary, including much shouting and yelling (on both sides no doubt). His onetime business manager, Douglas Urbanski, quit because of the constant run-ins with Moore. Those on the left who embrace him see him as a modern-day muckraker, whose goal is to incite outrage about important social issues. "Moore's anger has always been the fuel of his humor," wrote Britain's lefty *Guardian* newspaper.[23]

It is hard to find a liberal pundit who doesn't cater to the anger of the left—and with good reason. As we've seen, liberals tend to be angrier people than the general public.

Rallies against the World Trade Organization, the Iraq war, and for environmentalist causes often result in arrests for disorderly behavior. In August 2004, New York City cops arrested eighteen hundred demonstrators outside the Republican National Convention as the "calm, rational" left came to protest the "hate-filled" GOP. The liberal press spoke of "the cadre of activists desperate to unleash four years' worth of anger at the Bush administration." There were "hopes to make the Republicans' lives hell for as long as they're in New York." As one of the organizers bragged, they wanted to target GOP events with "anything from occupation to property destruction."[24] Meanwhile, outside that summer's Democratic National Convention, only a half dozen furious people were arrested during the entire week. Apparently, militantly pro-war Republicans are calmer than peace-loving antiwar Democrats.[25]

The cause of all this is not George W. Bush, nor is it a reaction to conservative talk radio. Since the sixties, modern liberals have embraced anger as a sign of genuine commitment to the cause. Since that tumultuous decade, liberalism has become dominated by those with intractable grievances. The liberal heroes of the era were the Chicago Seven, the Black Panthers, Students for a Democratic Society, and the National Organization for Women—all of which were fueled by anger and at times destructive rage. With various groups proclaiming their oppression, anger becomes justified, even necessary, in order to fight the injustice of the "system." Liberals talked about the need to "tell it like it is," with anger and verve when necessary.[26] The countercultural left loved individuals who dared to lash out in public—Abbie Hoffman, Gloria Steinem, Bella Abzug, Stokely Carmichael. Even the left's favorite comedians were angry—Lenny Bruce, George Carlin, Richard Pryor. Today, racism, sexism, homophobia, insensitivity, and a host of other words get tossed around with regularity and serve as a lubricant to the anger of the left.

Sixties radical Allen Ginsberg saw this and later remarked how destructive it was. He denounced what he called "the extreme one-dimensional politics of the New Left," which was based on "rising up angry." Rage was a mistake. "Any gesture made in anger is going to create more anger. Any gesture coming from rage and resentment creates more rage and resentment." Which is, of course, precisely what the left wants to accomplish.[27]

The left believes it is entitled to its anger in the name of numerous grievances. When women and ethnic minorities are angry at the social "oppression" they face, it is hailed as a form of authenticity. As Todd Gitlin, himself a man of the left, points out, "You can fall in love with your outrage."

Many on the liberal-left like to explain away acts of violence and rage. Richard Goldstein in the *Village Voice* claims that "air rage" and "road rage" are really the fault of corporations, because in "many interactions with a corporation, the balance of power has shifted away from the consumer." People are in a rage—and legitimately so. His solution? "Empower the regulators" to curtail corporate power.[28]

Feminists laud anger and aggression. Gloria Steinem spoke at the Feminist Expo in 2000 of "the gift of righteous anger" that allows women to have a "sense of self."[29] In her book *Moving Beyond Words,* Steinem wrote about "a healthy anger that . . . loosens my tongue, leaves me ever more impatient and energized." When feminist poet Audre Lorde died, she was praised for her "fearless rage." According to one writer, "Her anger is an act of self-love."[30]

A popular environmentalist group encourages those in the movement to "recharge our rage," and tells people that to protect the environment, "We need directed anger."[31]

After riots broke out in Seattle during a meeting of the World Trade Organization, *Dissent* magazine defended the rage in the streets. We need to "recognize ourselves in the anger we see on the streets," wrote Rachel Neumann and David

Glenn, and remind ourselves that "rage is a natural and required response."[32] A favorite slogan on the antiwar left today: "If you're not outraged, you're not paying attention."

The left has always placed a premium on anger. Norman Mailer in his book *The White Negro* was hopeful of a future in which "we are raging to be born." Mailer's personal life has likewise been full of rage: He stabbed his first wife with a pen, bit off part of actor Rip Torn's ear, head-butted Gore Vidal, challenged McGeorge Bundy to a fistfight, and threatened to flatten just about anyone who disagreed with him. He wrote to William Styron, with whom he was having a disagreement: "I will invite you to a fight in which I expect to stomp out of you a fat amount of your yellow and treacherous shit." He championed the cause of releasing murderer-turned-writer Jack Abbott from prison and praised those who commit violent crimes. In the introduction to one of Abbott's books he wrote: "Not only the worst of the young are sent to prison, but the best—that is, the proudest, the bravest, the most daring, the most enterprising, and the most undefeated of the poor." Mailer thought anger, rage, and violence were authentic expressions that should not be condemned out of hand. He typically "equated violence not only with virility but also with creativity and moral courage," as the *New York Times* put it. But the left—with the exception of a few feminists with whom he feuded—embraces Mailer as a glorious talent.[33]

Liberal excuses for violence perpetrated in the name of justified "rage" abound. In the sixties, mass murderer Charles Manson was upheld as a hero by many on the left because he was expressing his "legitimate rage." The Weathermen praised Manson as a folk hero. An underground newspaper in Los Angeles named Manson its "Man of the Year" in 1969. Jerry Rubin visited Manson in prison and declared that he was a great "inspiration."

When a deranged black man named Colin Ferguson walked onto a Long Island Rail Road commuter train in 1994 and shot twenty-five defenseless passengers, many on the left sprang to his defense. Defense attorney William Kunstler offered an excuse for the violence: "black rage." Apparently Ferguson was shooting white commuters because of rampant racism. (As Clarence Page pointed out at the time, this was more than a bit demeaning to blacks, implying they couldn't control themselves.)[34]

Mayor Coleman Young of Detroit explained away the riots and violence in his city on the grounds that it was a legitimate expression of anger. "Why do blacks look inward, and why do more blacks kill each other than whites?" he asked. "Well, it can be found in the simple statistic that in the United States black families earn exactly half or somewhat less than half of what whites earn."[35] In his sixties bestseller *Soul on Ice,* jailed Black Panther Eldridge Cleaver justified raping white women as an act of political rage.[36] Professor Cornel West, now of Princeton, offered a defense of the 1992 riots in Los Angeles after the Rodney King verdict, explaining that it was an understandable response to "self-serving notions of freedom and justice" put forward by whites.[37] When a horrified nation saw footage of truck driver Reginald Denny being brutally beaten by a mob—struck on the head with bricks, kicked, and punched to the point of near death—Representative Maxine Waters justified these actions as the result of anger and pent-up frustration.[38]

Perhaps this is what Jean-Paul Sartre meant when he praised anger and rage as a form of heroism: "irrepressive violence . . . is man re-creating himself."[39]

The lefty Foundation for Taxpayer and Consumer Rights even holds a "Rage for Justice" awards dinner every year at the Beverly Hills Hotel. The liberal outfit receives praise and support from the likes of Sen. Dianne Feinstein and actors Warren Beatty, Annette Bening, and Mike Farrell. When Elizabeth Edwards, wife of John Edwards, received the "Rage" award in 2007, she explained the need for liberals to embrace an "uncompromising rage" about the issues they care about. One simply can't imagine the National Rifle Association offering a "rage" award, with praises of righteous anger sung by Dick Cheney.

Mario Cuomo ran for office with the slogan "Put Your Anger to Work." Julian Bond of the NAACP noted the anger in the black community and asked: "How can anger be turned into action?"[40] Feminist Ann Marlowe, writing in the *Village Voice,* expresses an attitude that is all too common on the left: "Every day I hear or read things that make me angry for feminist reasons, but I don't know where to place the blame."[41]

This anger on the left is demonstrative, something to be shared with others. As Stephen Miller of the American Enterprise Institute points out, it is not a question of "private seething, nor is it focused primarily on an opponent. Rather, it is anger intended for display. It says, in effect, 'Look at me, I'm angry.' "[42] To understand this kind of behavior you don't need to be a psychologist, you need a degree in primatology.

Mild-mannered liberals such as E. J. Dionne of the *Washington Post* justify liberal anger in books such as *Stand Up and Fight Back.* Liberal blogger Glenn Greenwald and others encourage their comrades on the left to "embrace the anger." Paul Starobin, writing in the *Atlantic Monthly,* proclaims that liberal anger is an expression of the finest human impulses: "Liberal anger at its best is drawn from the deepest and purest source of all: love." (Next time an antiwar protester spits at you, remember: The saliva is offered in love.)[43]

A look at recent presidents and presidential candidates over the past quarter century offers a stark contrast. Ronald Reagan had a calm, sturdy disposition; even when his critics insulted and called him names, he would dismiss them with gentle humor. President George H. W. Bush was criticized by many for his lack of "vision," but few accused him of being an angry man. George W. Bush has his Texas swagger and Dick Cheney his secretive demeanor, but neither is known for fits of rage (though you might want to think twice before going on a hunting trip with Cheney). The only man to run as an "angry conservative" over the past thirty years was Pat Buchanan, and we saw how far that got him with conservative voters.

Those on the liberal side of the equation, on the other

hand, seem to covet their anger. Take Al Gore, often perceived as calm and steady. As Joe Klein of *Time* magazine pointed out during the 2000 election: "Gore's anger is personal. He is angry at Bill Clinton (yes, for Monica Lewinsky but also for being such an impossible act to follow). He has been angry at Hillary Clinton since 1993, when the elected Vice President found himself competing with the unelected Vice President for Bill Clinton's attention. He is angry with Joe Lieberman—and with the moderate Democratic Leadership Council—for criticizing the 'people vs. the powerful' theme of his 2000 campaign. He and Dick Gephardt have always been bitter rivals. And he probably doesn't like John Kerry or Wes Clark very much either."[44]

Over the past decade, Gore has given anger-laden speeches accusing Republicans of all sorts of offenses—racism, greed, bigotry, and lack of care for the environment. In 2004 he gave a vein-popping speech in front of the liberal activist group Moveon in which he accused the Bush administration of, among other things, "establishing an American gulag."[45] In another speech in Nashville, which NBC News called "an angry, sweaty shout," Gore attacked Bush as one of history's worst presidents.

Howard Dean, when he ran for president in 2004, was the consummate angry candidate. He made anger the central feature of his campaign, with the exception of a few days toward the end of the Iowa contest when he tried to adopt a more statesmanlike approach (a strategy he soon abandoned). The *Washington Post* captured his political rise perfectly with the headline "Return of the Angry Man." His own brother calls him "radioactive." Former DNC chairman Terry McAuliffe calls him "the human fire hydrant." Dean lost his lead when a campaign speech famously degenerated into an angry incoherent howl that affronted the national press, but he was rewarded for his anger. He was appointed head of the Democratic National Committee.

Hillary Clinton has a long history of demonstrative anger. She was famous in Arkansas for her "screaming fits," as Clinton friend Susan McDougal described them. Hillary's wrath was so strong that Bill had to "cower a bit," said John Brummett, a political reporter with the *Arkansas Gazette*. In another widely reported incident, she ripped the hinges off the kitchen door in the governor's mansion. Once in Washington, she was known to evoke fear in White House staffers, well aware there would be "hell to pay" if her wishes were ignored. When critics called her angry, Senator Clinton adroitly turned it into a virtue: "If they do that, wear it as a badge of honor, because you know what? There are lots of things that we should be angry and outraged about these days."[46]

Former President Clinton is also prone to flashes of anger. He has spoken openly about the "deeper, constant anger" that motivates and drives him to succeed. He becomes particularly upset when questioned by hostile media. Asked by a reporter for *Investor's Business Daily* about questionable campaign contributions from Chinese entities, Clinton reportedly launched into a tirade against RNC chairman Haley

Barbour, the FBI, Bob Dole, and Republicans in general. When Fox anchor Chris Wallace (a registered Democrat) asked him about his spotty counterterrorism record, Clinton went after "right-wingers, Fox News, Rupert Murdoch, and Karl Rove" while angrily jabbing his finger at Wallace.

Conservatives such as Ronald Reagan, George W. Bush, or Dick Cheney have faced equally blunt questioning and it's hard to find an instance where they even raised their voices. Conservatives can get angry and lash out, but they usually do it in private. After Sen. Patrick Leahy accused Vice President Dick Cheney of "cronyism" with regard to Halliburton, the two ran into each other on the Senate floor. Cheney ended the heated conversation with "Go f—— yourself."[47] But these are clear exceptions. As the World Values Survey points out, those on the left are much more likely to say they became "upset" when criticized compared to conservatives.

Eliot Spitzer, governor of New York until his ignoble fall for alleged involvement in a prostitution ring, had (much like his Democratic predecessor Mario Cuomo) a reputation for flashes of anger and lashing out at his political opponents. According to *New York* magazine, he told Republican minority leader James Tedisco: "I'm a f——ing steamroller, and I'll roll over you." He physically threatened members of the legislature and was reportedly prone to shouting at his staff, according to the article. His aides referred to these antics as "the full Spitzer." Far from apologizing for these outbursts, Spitzer declared them to be a good thing. "Outrage helps both create a conversation to frame issues and generate an understanding of the issues," Spitzer helpfully explained.[48]

Modern liberals see themselves as reformers intent on changing society, indeed the whole world, for the better. When others don't agree with them, they become suffused with righteous indignation. After all, these people are halting progress! Conservatives accept the fact that others may not share their views, but liberals often require others to agree with them in order to be treated with even minimal respect.

What makes modern liberalism so appealing is that it allows people to give free rein to their anger and outrage. Far from suppressing it—which is what traditional morality and religious faiths call for—liberalism considers anger a virtue, a sign of caring, concern, and genuine humanity. Liberal anger, you see, is really "love."

MIND WARS
Why Conservatives Actually Know More Than Liberals

odern liberalism often promotes a form of intellectual haughtiness, a presumption that liberals know more than others precisely because they are liberals. Many liberals believe that they are smarter than conservatives. If you don't believe me, just ask a liberal. George McGovern says flat out, "Just about every educated person I encounter in the world is a liberal."[1] Mario Cuomo, former governor of New York, claims that conservatives "write their messages in crayons" while liberals "use fine-point quills."[2]

Billionaire Ted Turner explained to a rally that conservatives are stupid: "People who think like us may be in the minority, but we're the smart ones." Those who disagree with his liberal politics are "a whole bunch of dummies." Democratic Party consultant Paul Begala maintains that conservatives are ignorant boobs while "Democrats are the children of the Enlightenment" (whatever that's supposed to mean). Mark Morford, a *San Francisco Chronicle* columnist, agrees and claims that conservatives are "far more unlikely than their liberal brethren to allow their kids to develop the capacity for independent thought."[3]

A columnist for the *Seattle Post-Intelligencer* explained that all the smart people are liberal. "Liberals are where the brains are, and the brains are where the liberals are. From a historical perspective, conservatives were the folks who clung to the idea that the earth was flat."[4] Former congressman Patricia Schroeder, now head of the Association of American Publishers, declared that Republicans are simpleminded: "The Karl Roves of the world have built a generation that just wants slogans: 'Don't raise my taxes; no new taxes.' " In contrast, Democrats "can't say anything in less than a paragraph. We really want the whole picture, want to peel the onion."[5] Professor Drew Westen has written a book arguing that the reason Democrats have lost in recent elections is that their arguments are too logical and the average American simply can't absorb so much serious thinking.[6]

Thomas Frank, in his *New York Times* bestseller *What's the Matter with Kansas?*, seeks to explain why rural voters in the heartland don't vote for liberal Democrats. His conclusion: They are simply too ignorant to recognize their own interests. Voting for conservative Republicans is not only a "species of derangement," it "is the bedrock of our civic order; it is the foundation on which all else rests." (Frank is that species of liberal Marxist who thinks economic issues trump the moral values that are fundamental to a good social order. He would do well to pay closer attention to these concerns, the better to grasp why they are indeed "the foundation on which all else rests.")[7]

Novelist Norman Mailer, in his book *The Big Empty,* posits that Republicans and Bush have joined forces in an axis of ignorance. "Karl Rove was there to recognize that there were substantial powers to be obtained by catering to stupid stubborn people, and George W. Bush would be the man to harvest such resources. George W. Bush understood stupid people well. They were not dumb, their minds were not crippled in any way. They had chosen to be stupid because that offered its own kind of power. To win a great many contests of will, they needed only to ignore all evidence. Bright people would break down trying to argue with them."[8] Bright people like Mailer of course.

James Wolcott, writing in *Vanity Fair,* attacks what he calls the ignorance of red states, claiming that of the "10 smartest states" in the country, 8 are blue. The red states are "a solid bloc of recalcitrant dunces," he claims. How did he come to that conclusion? He used statistics from the Morgan Quinto Press, which determined the smartest states based on their spending on public education, teacher salaries, and other factors. (Yes, that is correct: Intelligence and knowledge are now determined by how much the government spends on education. This is in many ways the liberal stance par excellence.)[9]

A recent study by a couple of academics claimed to show that liberals are smarter, better capable of dealing with "informational complexity." The story was picked up by news outlets around the world, including Australian National Radio and *The Guardian* in London. The *Los Angeles Times* concluded that the study provided evidence that "liberals might be better judges of the facts than conservatives." How did the researchers come to this profound conclusion? They took a group of students and had them push a button on a computer when they saw the letter "W" as opposed to the letter "M" on the screen.[10]

The "liberals are smarter" meme is also a handy way of explaining liberal dominance at our colleges and universities. Study after study has established that the majority of college professors are liberal, vote for Democratic candidates, and often openly despise the few conservatives in their midst. Although this obvious truth was denied for many years as a conservative canard, the evidence is now so overwhelming that most liberals no longer bother to deny it. Still, the question remains: Why are so many faculty members liberal? The answer (to liberals at any rate) is simple: Conservatives just aren't smart enough to cut it in academe. "We try to hire the best, smartest people available," says Professor Robert Brandon, chair of the Philosophy Department at Duke. "If, as

John Stuart Mill said, stupid people are generally conservative, then there are lots of conservatives we will never hire. . . . Players in the NBA tend to be taller than average. There is a good reason for this. Members of academia tend to be a bit smarter than average. There is a good reason for this, too."[11]

Professor Michael Berube, a darling of the liberal-left intelligentsia, says the dominance by liberals is natural because "conservatism in America becomes more and more associated with the know-nothing, Tom DeLay wing of the Republican Party."[12] Professor Brian Leiter, who teaches philosophy at the University of Texas, explains that "the Republican Party has gone increasingly bonkers, such that educated and informed people by and large can't stomach it anymore."[13]

Ted Jelen, a University of Nevada, Las Vegas, professor of political science, simply asserts that "liberals are smarter." "I'm quite serious," Mr. Jelen said. "The Republican Party has taken some outrageous positions on issues like abortion and free speech, and has in effect priced itself out of the intellectual market."[14] Needless to say, the few open conservatives in academe are subject to constant abuse. The esteemed historian John Moser went to a meeting of the Organization of American Historians and made the mistake of mentioning that he voted for George W. Bush. One colleague was stunned. "And yet you write books. . . ."[15]

This sense of intellectual superiority trickles down to rank-and-file liberals. According to the American National Election Study, self-described liberals are more likely to claim that they are "better informed about government" than other Americans. Self-assured liberals are confident of their intellectual superiority. At Stanford University, a group of conservatives and liberals were asked how well they knew their own arguments and those of their political opponents. Liberals were much more likely to claim that they could "predict each other's views" and better understood their opponents than the other way around. (News flash: The researchers did not find that to be the case.)

Liberals have a lot of emotion invested in the idea that they are smarter than conservatives. Their assumption is clear: Simply by embracing modern liberalism they have proven themselves to be of superior intellect. But the reality is otherwise. Authoritative studies show that conservatives are actually better informed, more knowledgeable, and better educated than liberals. Allow me to present the evidence.

During the 2000 election, George W. Bush was often given the moniker "stupid." A Boston television reporter tripped him up with a "pop quiz," asking him the names of foreign leaders. At the same time his opponent, Vice President Al Gore, was presented as the consummate intellectual. He went out of his way to drop phrases like "Cartesian revolution" and used complex metaphors like "the clockwork universe" in his speeches.

Indeed, Gore seemed obsessed with proving how smart he was—and the media was his willing accomplice. The media reported at least a dozen times that Gore was "the smartest kid in the class." Bloomberg News observed that Gore had little patience for those "a few IQ points short of genius." The *New York Times* asked (in all seriousness), "Is Gore too smart to be president?" His biggest challenge, the paper explained, was "to show that he is a regular guy despite a perceived surplus of gravitas, which at least some Americans seem to find intimidating." This liberal assumption that a candidate can be just too darn smart to win a presidential election in this country goes back to Adlai Stevenson.[16]

What proof was there of Gore's alleged gravitas? How exactly did the media know that Gore was so smart and Bush so dumb? In fact, the record did not indicate any of this was true. It was often alleged, probably with reason, that Bush only got into Yale because his father had gone there and his grandfather had been a Connecticut senator. Yet Gore, with high school B's and C's (his only A's were in art), got into Harvard in part because (like other politicians' sons, including a raft of Kennedys) his father was a famous senator. At Harvard, Gore's grades did not improve. In his sophomore year he earned a D, a C-minus, two Cs, two C-pluses, and one B-minus. He was in the bottom fifth of his class his first two years in school. Later he flunked out of divinity school (failing five of his eight classes) and dropped out of Vanderbilt University Law School.[17] Gore was once asked (after having served in the U.S. Senate for several years) to name his favorite president. "President Knox," he replied.

Sen. John Kerry, when he ran against George W. Bush in

2004, was likewise heralded as an intellectual in contrast to the ill-informed Bush. It started in 1999, when Kerry "questioned Mr. Bush's intelligence," as the *New York Times* put it. "All over this country people are asking whether or not George Bush is smart enough to be president of the United States," Kerry said. During the 2004 campaign he continued with that theme, supported by the Democratic Party, liberal commentators, and the mainstream news media. Howell Raines, former executive editor of the *New York Times,* explained during the election that it was quite obvious that Bush was a dim bulb in contrast to Kerry: "Does anyone in America doubt that Kerry has a higher IQ than Bush? I'm sure the candidates' SATs and college transcripts would put Kerry far ahead."[18]

Fact checking was apparently not necessary for Raines. Though at the time, of course, no one could actually check because Kerry kept refusing to release his transcripts from Yale, or any information about intelligence tests that he would have taken as a navy officer. Bush had taken the equivalent Air Force Qualifying Test, and they would have made a good point of comparison. But the results were not, Kerry said, "relevant" to the campaign, even though his campaign was based in part on Bush's lack of intelligence. (A similar excuse was made in regard to Kerry's military records, though his campaign was largely based on his claim to have been a hero in Vietnam—before he became an outspoken critic of the war. In other words, he was for the war before he was against it.)

Then a navy veteran named Sam Sewell noticed something on the Kerry campaign website. In one of the documents posted on the web page, an obscure military report offered a cryptic score that was actually the result of an IQ-like qualifying test Kerry had taken in 1966. As it happened, George W. Bush had taken the same test just a few years later. Columnist Steve Sailer determined that Bush's score put him in the 95th percentile, giving him an IQ in the 120s. Kerry's score was slightly lower, putting him in the 91st percentile.[19]

When these results became public, NBC's Tom Brokaw asked Kerry about them. He was more than a bit peeved. Kerry dodged the question and wondered out loud how they became public in the first place. "I don't know how they've done it, because my record is not public," he told Brokaw. "So I don't know where you're getting that from." A few days later, on the Don Imus show, Brokaw revealed just how much it had bugged Kerry that he had been beaten by Bush on the IQ test. After the cameras stopped rolling, Brokaw recalled, Kerry explained, "I must have been drinking the night before I took that military aptitude test."

After Bush won reelection, it became clear why Kerry hadn't wanted to release his college records. The *Boston Globe* discovered that Bush actually had higher grades at Yale and also had higher SAT scores. (Bush's scores were also higher than those of Sen. Bill Bradley, another liberal often described as learned and brilliant.)[20]

But the "conservatives are dunces" mantra goes well beyond George W. Bush. Liberals take it for granted—literally—

that Democratic presidents are brighter than Republicans. Ronald Reagan was famously called an "amiable dunce" by Clark Clifford, an opinion widely shared among the Georgetown social set. *Doonesbury* creator (and former Yalie) Garry Trudeau even wrote a play about what an ignoramous Reagan was. President George H. W. Bush, despite having graduated from Yale in two and a half years, was likewise dismissed as a buffoon.

In 2001 the Lovenstein Institute released a report claiming scientific proof that liberal presidents were more intelligent than their Republican counterparts. In a press release, the institute claimed that Bill Clinton had an Einsteinlike IQ of 182, followed closely by Jimmy Carter and JFK. The Republicans? George H. W. Bush might have been Phi Beta Kappa at Yale, but his IQ was a below-average 98. Lower still were those dunces, Eisenhower and Reagan. George W. Bush (with degrees from Yale and Harvard) was borderline retarded. His IQ was said to be 91—literally half that of Clinton's.[21]

A few months later, another study emerged demonstrating that the average IQ of states that had voted for Gore was much higher than those that went for Bush. Connecticut was given an average IQ of 113, while conservative Utah scored an 87. (Again, barely above retarded.) According to these numbers, the 16 smartest states all went for Kerry, while the 26 dumbest went for Bush.[22]

These sensational findings seemingly confirmed what many in the media already believed. Trudeau ran a *Doones-*

bury strip about it. *The Economist* magazine, the *St. Petersburg Times,* London's *Daily Mirror,* radio talk show hosts, and liberal bloggers eagerly ran with the story. Urbandude.com typified the liberal attitude when he smugly noted, "I've got a Mensa certified IQ of 132." But apparently he wasn't smart enough: Both studies were complete fictions. ("Alas, we were victims of a hoax," admitted *The Economist.* "No such data exists.")[23]

The curious thing is how easily these findings were accepted by some in the media. Imagine if someone had published a report claiming that conservatives had much higher IQs than liberals. Would newspapers and commentators run such a story uncritically? To the contrary, they would likely first check on the results and subject the findings to serious scrutiny. In short, the bias in favor of "smart liberals" seems widely accepted in our society.

Popular culture has greatly contributed to the myth of ignorant conservatives and enlightened liberals. One study by a group of academics found that by examining 124 characters in 47 popular political films spanning five decades, liberals were routinely depicted as "more intelligent, friendly, and good" than conservatives.[24]

The arrogance of some liberals in this regard is astonishing. You don't even have to be highly educated yourself to complain about how uneducated conservatives are. Michael Moore, college dropout, travels all over Europe talking about how "idiotic and uneducated" conservatives are. He also said: "Once you settle for a Ronald Reagan, then it's easy to settle for a George Bush, and once you settle for a George Bush, then it's real easy to settle for Bush II. You know, this should be evolution, instead it's deevolution. What's next?"[25]

Professor Bruce Fleming, a self-professed liberal, explains this liberal attitude perfectly. "All of us are ignorant of many things. It's just that the liberal here thinks s/he knows what the conservative is ignorant of."[26]

This sublime confidence in their own superiority leads to a closed-minded insistence that liberals know what is right. Scholars at Stanford, the University of Illinois, and Williams conducted four studies on the subject of "asymmetric insight." Basically, this is the notion that some people claim to know more than others. Surveys were conducted with hundreds of students. Among their findings: Liberals are much more likely to believe that their knowledge of conservatives and their arguments surpasses that of conservatives themselves. The results were similar when it came to the abortion issue. Abortion rights advocates claimed to have greater knowledge and insight than those who are pro-life.[27]

There are no studies that directly evaluate IQ and political orientation. But there are many other tools that measure knowledge and intelligence. And nothing beats a survey that asks people specific questions to test their general knowledge.

Consistently over the past two decades, studies show that conservatives are more knowledgeable than liberals when it comes to basic political facts. Some of the knowledge gaps are funny. During the 2000 election, for example, the American National Election Study found that 10 percent of self-described liberals thought Sen. Joe Lieberman, Al Gore's running mate, was a "Baptist." (No conservatives made that mistake.) By nearly 20 percent, conservatives bested liberals in correctly identifying Lieberman as Jewish. At the same time, 12 percent of liberals said that Al Gore was Jewish. (Only 1 percent of conservatives made that mistake.) A lot of liberals didn't even know which state Lieberman was from. Conservatives bested liberals by nearly 10 points in correctly identifying him as the senator from Connecticut. Same for Al Gore: Conservatives correctly identified Tennessee as his home state 79 percent of the time, while only 65 percent of self-identified liberals got that right.[28]

The results were similar during the 2004 election. When asked to identify William Rehnquist of the Supreme Court and Vice President Dick Cheney, conservatives again bested liberals. (Apparently there are those on the left who absolutely *hate* Dick Cheney—they just don't know who he is.)[29]

So liberals are smarter than conservatives, and confident that they know more about politics. But they are less likely to know the names of their senators. The Social Capital Survey found that conservatives bested both liberals and moderates when asked that question. Conservatives also have a better grasp of how our government and Constitution are supposed to work. Another survey asked, "Who determines if a law is constitutional?" Conservatives were more likely to get the answer right (the Supreme Court). When asked, "How many terms can a president serve?" conservatives also got the answer right more often than liberals, as they did to the question, "How many votes are needed in Congress to override a presidential veto?"[30]

When Democrat pollster Peter Hart asked voters whether they knew if Supreme Court justices served lifetime terms, Republicans beat Democrats by 10 percentage points.[31]

During every election, the American National Election Study has asked basic questions about American politics. Conservatives always seem to get more answers correct than their often self-assured liberal neighbors. Which party controls the U.S. Senate (conservatives win by 9 points), which controls the House of Representatives (conservatives by 5 points), correctly name the speaker of the House (conservatives by 6 points). Conservatives were also twice as likely to know how many years their incumbent congressman had been in office.[32]

Conservatives were 20 points more likely to recall the names of both candidates who were running for Congress in their district, and the names of their senators. Surprisingly enough—even to some conservatives—the National Election Study found that the more you listen to Rush Limbaugh, the more knowledgeable you are about politics. Those who listened every day were 20 percent more likely to be able to name both congressional candidates in their district than those who listened only occasionally or not at all. I guess all the smart people don't necessarily listen to NPR.[33]

One of the great myths in American politics today is that talk radio listeners are poorly educated robots who traffic in ignorant prejudice. Academic studies show that the opposite is true. People who *don't* listen to talk radio tend to be "less well educated than listeners," found one study. "Political talk radio exposure was associated with greater faith in people, lower authoritarianism."[34]

In the 2000 election, each political group was given a ranking based on how well it did on the political knowledge test. Ilya Somin, law professor at George Mason University, created a table based on the results. It was posted on a website run by UCLA law professor Eugene Volokh.[35] (I double-checked and confirmed Somin's findings.) Here are the results:

Strong Republican	18.7
Independent-Republican	15.7
Strong Democrat	15.4
Independent-Democrat	14.2
Weak Republican	14.1
Weak Democrat	13.3
Independent	9.5

As Somin points out, the three-point gap between Strong Republican and Strong Democrat is the equivalent of several years of formal education. The survey also explodes the myth that Independents are choosy because they are somehow more thoughtful and better informed than strict party-line voters.

When you look at what young people know, a similar gap emerges. Young conservatives are better informed about politics than those on the left. The Pew Research Center asked young people in 2006 basic questions like, "Which political party has the majority in Congress?" Those who called themselves "very conservative" beat those who were "very liberal" by more than 20 points.[36] A study by professors at Duke and the University of North Carolina found similar results when they compared students at conservative "fundamentalist" schools and those in public high schools. After surveying students at more than ten schools, they found that the conservative students had significantly higher scores when it came to "political knowledge."[37]

The claim of superior liberal knowledge simply does not conform to the facts. Surveys consistently demonstrate that conservatives and/or Republicans are more knowledgeable about political affairs. But that doesn't stop liberals from believing they can do a better job of running the country. When asked "Could you do a good job in public office?" liberals are more likely to agree strongly with that statement than conservatives, who actually seem to know more about how government works.[38]

There are other measures that follow a similar pattern. The General Social Surveys ask people regularly about their general knowledge. Looking at the data over a ten-year period, you find that with occasional fluctuations, Republicans average almost one more year of education than Democrats, and tend to have a higher final degree. The surveys also asked people a series of simple word tests. The highest score in this basic vocabulary test came from conservative Republicans. Democrats scored very near the bottom on both the vocabulary and analogy tests. People were given a word and then a series of words, one of which was clearly associated with it. (Given the word "beast," they would be offered the words "afraid," "words," "large," "animal," or "separate." The correct answer would be "animal.") Strong Republicans did the best, outscoring both independents and Strong Democrats. Fifty-one percent of Strong Democrats missed half or more of the ten questions. Only 30 percent of Republicans did.[39]

These numbers fluctuate from year to year depending on how people identify themselves. But there can be little doubt that Republicans tend to be better informed and educated than their Democratic counterparts.[40]

The same holds true for economics. Professor Alan S. Blinder of Princeton University conducted a study in conjunction with the Brookings Institution in an effort to find out what people know about basic economics and their attitudes toward several issues. Blinder, who served on President Clinton's Council of Economic Advisers, surveyed more than one thousand people. What he found was that those who supported George W. Bush's tax cuts, free trade, and deregulation knew more about economics than others. "Respondents with higher levels of general economic knowledge," he found, were "less likely to favor tax hikes." "More-educated people" were also more likely to "favor partial privatization" of Social Security, another conservative policy goal.[41]

. . .

Liberals love to snicker at conservatives because they tend to be more religious. And for the modern liberal, faith and ignorance often go hand in hand.

Michael Weisskopf, then of the *Washington Post,* captured the prevailing attitude among media liberals when he wrote some years ago that religious conservatives are "largely poor, uneducated, and easy to command." *60 Minutes* fixture Andy Rooney says that Americans' religious faith is best explained by "a lack of education": "They haven't been exposed to what the world has to offer." Garry Wills published an essay after Bush's reelection in 2004 titled "the End of the Enlightenment" because he received so many votes from religious people: "Can a people that believe more fervently in the Virgin Birth than in evolution still be called an Enlightened nation?" Nicholas Kristof, a columnist for the *New York Times,* echoed that sentiment. "The faith in the Virgin Birth reflects the way American Christianity is becoming less intellectual and more mystical over time."[42]

Chris Hedges, a former reporter for the *New York Times,* has written an alarmist book about the religious right called *American Fascists.* His argument is that Americans cling to Christianity out of superstition and a need for blind faith in something. Apparently liberals are more rational than conservatives, whose thinking is guided by tradition and superstition.[43]

This is a grotesque parody of reality. Conservatives do

tend to adhere to Judeo-Christian teaching more than liberals. It is a fact, for instance, that more conservatives (83 percent) believe in heaven and hell than self-described liberals (68 percent). But this does not make conservatives anti-intellectual. Faith and belief are not inconsistent with sound thinking. Indeed, as G. K. Chesterton pointed out nearly a century ago, if you reject traditional religious convictions, you don't replace them with nothing—you replace them with *anything*. Secular liberals need to put their faith in something, so they tend to gravitate toward superstition—ghosts, ESP, and other "paranormal phenomena."

A Gallup Survey found that 42 percent of liberals believe in ghosts—but only 25 percent of conservatives. A CBS poll found similar results, including the fact that 43 percent of liberals believe we can communicate with the spirits of dead people, compared with 29 percent of conservatives. Liberals were also much more likely to believe in ESP, telepathy, astrology, witches, reincarnation, and channeling than conservatives. Liberals are almost three times as likely to believe that they have lived a previous life, and almost twice as likely to have consulted a fortune teller or psychic. They believe in witches and haunted houses by more than 10 points over conservatives. They were almost 20 points more likely to say that UFOs have visited the earth; and to round out the list, those on the left were more likely to be superstitious about black cats, walking under a ladder, the number 13, breaking a mirror, and knocking on wood.[44]

Another survey in New Jersey found that 53 percent of

liberals believe in ghosts. (That was actually a higher percentage than those who believed "Bill and Hillary Clinton like each other.")[45] Often forgotten in this discussion is that for years, urbane, liberal, and sophisticated Berkeley, California, has posted the highest circulation figures for that thoughtful, reality-based journal, Dell's *Horoscope* magazine.[46]

As we saw earlier, liberals make up the bulk of those who inhabit the New Age movement. The left has always been less concerned and judgmental about religious cults than conservatives, viewing them as just alternative belief systems. The rise of cults in the 1970s never really created much of a stir on the left. Indeed, in some instances it endorsed or lent credibility to these movements. Should it surprise anyone that when Jim Jones and his suicidal cult arrived in Guyana in 1978, they came with a fistful of references from the liberal-left, including Bella Abzug, Vice President Walter Mondale, Roy Wilkins, and half a dozen others?[47]

The religious convictions of conservatives such as Ronald Reagan and George W. Bush have always been seen as one of the reasons they lack intellect. The *New Republic* branded Bush and his administration "instinctive and anti-intellectual," in large part because of Bush's religious faith. The *New York Times'* Paul Krugman claims that the Republican Party is "dominated by people who believe truth should be determined by revelation, not research."[48] Ronald Reagan was derided because he believed in the biblical notion of an apocalypse. When John Ashcroft was up for Senate confirmation as attorney general, many openly wondered whethe his Pentecostal convictions would lead him to impose a theocracy. But when equally fervent religious or spiritual convictions are espoused by leading figures on the left, you never hear the same sort of criticism.

Hillary Clinton is "widely praised as brilliant," noted *Forbes* magazine in a profile, and she has certainly never been criticized as "anti-intellectual."[49] Yet Senator Clinton not only professes belief in her Methodist faith but has entertained a number of eccentric spiritual ideas. During the 1990s she was a devoted reader of James Redfield's *The Celestine Prophecy,* a novel supposedly based on ancient Mayan texts—which actually don't exist. In the book, Redfield promises a new Eden, where truth will be accessible to all and people will simply "intuit" the solution to global problems of war and peace. As we evolve, moreover, we will begin to vibrate at higher levels, making us invisible to lower beings.

Clinton has also been an admirer of New Age guru Deepak Chopra, who believes that "aging is simply learned behavior." (Tell that to your ninety-year-old grandfather!) Chopra slept in the Lincoln Bedroom and was a guest at White House state dinners during the Clinton administration. He is currently a member of Indian Americans for Hillary and a financial supporter of her presidential campaign. Chopra believes that the magic of Merlin is *real,* and in *The Seven Spiritual Laws of Success* he promises "the ability to create unlimited wealth with effortless ease." To achieve supreme health, he encourages people to cross over into the "fourth dimension," where the body is a mere illusion.[50] Nothing irrational here!

In 2005, Hillary hired Gia Medeiros as a consultant to her Hill PAC and "Friends of Hillary" Senate campaign. Medeiros was paid $75,000 for a research project—but she was no political consultant. She had made a name for herself as "an unconventional corporate teen-marketing guru who believes the supernatural can be used to pitch products to young people." (She was later fired, not because of her mystical mumbo jumbo, but because of some impolitic comments she made about 9/11 families.)[51]

When President Clinton lost Congress in 1994, he summoned no fewer than five New Age gurus to help him "search for a way back." These included Marianne Williamson, "sacred psychologist" Jean Houston, and Mary Catherine Bateson, an anthropologist who studies "nontraditional life paths." Houston explained that she could sense Hillary's tension because of the failed health care plan. "Being Hillary Clinton was like being Mozart with his hands cut off," she explained. The first lady was "carrying the burden of 5,000 years of history when women were subservient. . . . She was reversing thousands of years of expectations and was there up front, probably more than virtually any woman in human history—apart from Joan of Arc."

Over the next six months Hillary met with Houston and Bateson and talked with long-dead historical figures who would "understand her travails" and help her "achieve self-healing." Sitting in the White House solarium around a circular table, Hillary chatted with Eleanor Roosevelt (her "spiritual archetype") and Mahatma Gandhi ("a powerful symbol of stoic self-denial").[52]

More recently, Bill Clinton has embraced the teachings of New Age guru Ken Wilber, a self-described "transpersonal psychologist." Wilber, who was once a disciple of cult leader Da Free John, embraces the Indian philosophy of Nagarjuna and uses Buddhist meditation techniques to find what he calls "integral consciousness." Wilber brags that he has special insights and abilities. Even the Dalai Lama, he says, can't sustain "nondual awareness through deep sleep" like he can (whatever that means).

Clinton was introduced to Wilber's writing in early 1999 when he read *The Marriage of Sense and Soul.* The book argues that body, soul, mind, and matter all merge in a "great chain of being." Clinton sent Wilber a handwritten letter of praise and gave a copy of the book to Vice President Al Gore. Gore was equally impressed and later declared it to be "one of my favorite new books."[53] Gore later incorporated some of Wilber's ideas into his film *An Inconvenient Truth.*[54]

At the World Economic Forum in 2006, Clinton was asked by Klaus Schwab, founder of the WEF: "If you look at the world today, what are the three most important worries which you have?" Clinton responded: "If ordinary people don't perceive that our grand ideas are working in their lives, then they can't develop the higher level of consciousness, if I can use a kind of touchy-feely word, that American philosopher Ken Wilber wrote a whole book about, called *A Theory of Everything*. He said, you know, the problem is the world needs to be more integrated but it requires a consciousness that's way up there. . . . So I worry about that." Imagine if George W. Bush had gone to Davos and quoted from Saint Augustine—or even an evangelical minister. He would have been ridiculed.

Former president Jimmy Carter is a born-again Christian, but that has not stopped his left-wing admirers from proclaiming his brilliance. Norman Mailer, who considered Bush's faith to be evidence that he is a bumpkin, considered Carter "a genius."[55] Carter also professes belief in several occult phenomena that have not led anyone to question his intelligence. He claims to have seen a UFO "as bright as the moon" in the skies over Leary, Georgia. After determining that his brother Billy had nothing to do with it, Carter reported it as a flying saucer. The light was later identified as the planet Venus, which was more visible in the night sky on that day due to a planetary phenomenon.[56]

The Carters also claimed to have occupied a "haunted house." "I heard something in the attic every night that sent shivers up my spine," Rosalynn Carter explained to a newspaper. She saw "flashing lights in the attic when there was nobody in the house."[57] Yet Carter is lionized by the liberal left because, of course, he possesses the correct politics.

There are plenty of smart people who embrace both conservative and liberal philosophies—and plenty of stupid ones, too. But the conceit that somehow liberals are inherently more intellectual than conservatives simply does not hold up. What is curious is why liberals spend so much time trying to make this case. Perhaps it is because their ideology is predicated on the assumption that they are smarter. Liberals support affirmative action, the redistribution of wealth, control of the education curriculum, and a long list of social engineering projects. All of this rests on the assumption that they know best how to manage the lives of their fellow citizens. Conservative opposition is dismissed as irrational, wicked, or just plain stupid—anything but pragmatic or principled.

Part of the seductive appeal of modern liberalism is that it offers the answers to everything. There is something powerful about a political philosophy that says if you embrace me, you will prove your mental superiority because you have seen the light.

7.

WHINE COUNTRY
Or, Why Liberals Complain More

When Bill Clinton was president of the United States, leader of the free world, indeed, the most powerful man in the world, he did a lot of . . . well . . . whining. During his first term he whined about how mean people were on talk radio, the fact that he was broke, and that he was generally treated badly by the media, Congress, and just about everybody. He complained that he was tired, had "never worked so hard in his life," and that his wife was facing unfair scrutiny. George Stephanopoulos, his former aide, recalls Clinton pouting in the Oval Office because, in Clinton's estimation, no president had ever been treated as badly as he had. (Presumably he had forgotten about Garfield, Lincoln, Kennedy, and McKinley—presidents who were *assassinated* while in office.)[1]

Two weeks into his second term, Clinton compared his plight to that of Richard Jewell, the security guard falsely accused of setting off the 1996 Olympic Park bombs in Atlanta. He whined that Republicans raised more money than he did, and that he was not appreciated enough by pundits and critics. Sure, he was president of the United States, but he was president at the *wrong time.* "I would have much preferred being president during World War II," he offered at one point. "I'm a person out of my time."[2]

Weeks later, Clinton complained that the Republicans were just too mean. In 1997 he told the National Prayer Breakfast: "I remember when I came here one time, I got so mad at our friends in Congress and the Republican Party because they were real mean to me over something." (Can you imagine Dick Cheney complaining that someone was "mean" to him?) When the Monica Lewinsky matter blew up, he blamed the media, he blamed several women, and he blamed his political opponents. When he was forced to admit that he had, in fact, lied to a federal grand jury, Clinton complained that the Arkansas Bar Association had the gall to suspend his law license. "It's not right," he told NBC News.

President Clinton was not alone in his complain-a-thon. First Lady Hillary Clinton amassed a similarly impressive record of public whining while in Washington. First she griped that the American people "expect so much from the woman who is married to the president." When she was criticized for being too involved with policy, she whined that she would have to "put a bag" over her head to satisfy her critics. She indignantly demanded a "zone of privacy" over the Lewinsky scandal, and then accepted an $8 million book deal to write about it.

Complaining happens everywhere, both in and out of politics. Weeks after he beat Barry Goldwater, LBJ groused, "Nobody loves Johnson."[3] But the Clintons took the practice to new heights. In 2000, as he prepared to leave the White House, Clinton whined to the *New York Times* about how "hurt" and "bewildered" he was because Al Gore had not invited him to take part in his campaign. After the Clintons packed their bags and moved to Chappaqua, Clinton complained to *New York* magazine that his presidency was cut short in its prime, that he was just minutes away from sealing a deal in the Middle East, fixing Social Security, and solving race relations. He talked about imagined slights and complained that George W. Bush never sought him out for advice. When Clinton turned sixty, he even complained that he was getting too old too fast. He told *Rolling Stone* that he "never" got credit for his accomplishments. And when Fox reporter Chris Wallace asked him about his counterterrorism record, Clinton famously jabbed a finger in his face and accused him of a "conservative hit job."

Little surprise that *Time* magazine felt compelled to explain the "uncomfortable truth" about Clinton: "The President of the U.S., the most powerful man in the world, is a whiner."[4]

Some saw Clinton's chronic complaining as evidence that the baby boomers had finally arrived. Hopelessly self-centered, Clinton seemed to embody a whole generation accustomed to getting what they want. But certainly this is not true of many baby boomers. Can one imagine George W. Bush complaining that he was president at the wrong time? Or Rudy Giuliani comparing himself to a falsely accused security guard? What is at work here is not so much Clinton's age as his political beliefs.

Modern liberalism has become obsessed with victimization. There are of course real victims. But liberalism's embrace of victimology as a means to electoral victory means pretty much anyone can make such a claim. Political scientist Aaron Wildavsky calculates that victims now account for 374 percent of the population. Today the liberal-left is dominated by groups making claims of victim status—blacks, Hispanics, Asians, Native Americans, unwed mothers, artists, pampered academics, environmental activists, the poor, the unemployed, animal rights activists, women, homosexuals—all make the claim and receive considerable support from their comrades in suffering. The Wisconsin Department of Labor and Human Relations has even classified people with "offensive body odor" as handicapped under the state's Fair Employment Act—but for some reason they don't seem to get invited to many events.[5] Liberalism, that is to say, has a vested interest in being permanently aggrieved. As Kenneth Minogue argues in his classic book *The*

Liberal Mind, modern liberalism is completely wrapped up in "suffering situations" and grievances. When a modern liberal "defines himself as a victim," writes Julius Lester, he has "found a way to keep himself in a perpetual state of righteous self-pity and anger."[6]

Victimhood holds many advantages. As Charles Sykes points out in *A Nation of Victims,* by definition the victim is *always* innocent; the victim has moral authority. It is victim status, therefore, that justifies a smorgasbord of government entitlements and special privileges to ameliorate the victim's suffering. Of course there are plenty of specific entitlements and benefits offered to victims.

When Bill Clinton claimed, "I feel your pain," he was appealing to the victim classes in society.

Liberalism has become a belief system of complaint, entitlement, and dissatisfaction. Liberals have fostered a culture of whining and complaint designed to encourage Americans to embrace their inner victim. Doing so means expressing dissatisfaction toward just about everything in their lives. Liberal writer Michael Crowley openly admits as much when he says of the Democratic Party: "What does define and unify the party is a sense of victimhood."[7] Self-described liberal Wendy Kaminer likewise captured this spirit in an *Atlantic Monthly* essay: "Personally, I reserve the right to complain and even whine about whatever injustices are visited upon me—bad haircuts, bad boyfriends, and bad reviews. I have always believed in complaining—and in one view, that makes me a liberal."[8]

Kaminer's observation is not without an objective foundation. Many modern liberals are an unhappy lot, often disappointed with life. For them, the glass is always half empty. A survey by Pew Research, for example, found that 45 percent of Republicans reported being "very happy" compared with just 30 percent of Democrats. For those who might reply that this merely reflects disparities in wealth, keep in mind that even when controlling for income, Republicans are happier. Among individuals making over $75,000 per year, 52 percent of Republicans are "very happy" compared to only 41 percent of Democrats. Among those making less than $30,000 per year, it's 30 percent of Republicans and 23 percent of Democrats.

A look at the leading lights among conservatives and liberals seems to confirm this view. Compare Senators Harry Reid and Al Gore with Rudy Giuliani and George W. Bush. Who seems happier? As Stephen Hayward of the American Enterprise Institute puts it, many leaders on the political left have the demeanor of morticians, not inspiring political leaders.[9] Another survey found a 20-point difference between conservatives and liberals responding to the question, "How satisfied are you with life these days?" Sixty-six percent of conservatives said they were "very satisfied" compared with only 46 percent of liberals.[10]

The American National Election Study asked Americans how satisfying their life was. Only 12 percent of liberals said "completely satisfying" compared to 29 percent of conservatives. Twenty-four percent of liberals said life was "not very satisfying" compared to only 13 percent of conservatives.[11]

Modern liberals like to project the impression that they lead exciting lives in comparison to dull, buttoned-down conservatives. Conservatives are often put in the category of a modern-day Willy Loman: claustrophobic, sexually repressed, and profoundly depressed in their tiny cage. Liberals on the other hand are all about freedom and uplifting ideals, and they have all the fun. But the truth is otherwise. In fact, Republicans are generally more excited by life: 54 percent say life is exciting compared to only 43 percent of Democrats. Even when they have the same income, Republicans still come out ahead.

Some might say this only proves that ignorance is bliss. Unaware or unconcerned about the terrible injustices in the world, conservatives (according to liberal myth) are cloistered in their country club–style cocoons. Yet the facts prove exactly the opposite. When people are asked, for example, how often they think about deep questions such as "the meaning of life," the World Values Survey found that conservatives are 12 percent more likely to say "often" than self-described liberals.[12]

But many liberals are not just unhappy, they are chronically dissatisfied with virtually every aspect of their lives—job, money, family. In contrast, conservatives are much more content.

Consider the issue of jobs and career. The General Social

Surveys found liberals almost three times as likely to say they were dissatisfied with their jobs when compared to conservatives. By contrast, 53 percent of conservatives said they loved their jobs, compared with 41 percent of liberals. When modern liberals take time off, things don't seem to go much better. Another survey revealed that Democrats are much less happy with their hobbies than Republicans. Fully 63 percent of Republicans enjoyed their hobbies compared with only 51 percent of Democrats.

Liberal grousing extends to income as well. Liberals are much less happy with the amount of money they make—even when they earn the same amount as conservatives. The Social Capital Survey found, for example, that among middle-income earners, liberals were more than three times as likely to say they were "not at all satisfied" when compared to conservatives. Liberals were also much more likely to consider themselves poor—even when they are not. They are almost twice as likely as conservatives to classify their family income as "far below average" or "below average"—even when they earn the same income and are middle class.

But it's not just work *outside* the home that gets liberals grumbling; work *inside* the home tends to irritate them, too. Take something that no one really likes, such as housework. In study after study, Democrats are much more likely to complain that the division of work in their home "is unfair to me" than Republicans. In fact, they are *five times* as likely to whine about it. When asked how much housework their spouse did, Democrats were three times as likely to say "very little or none."[13] But while Democrats huffed about housework, Republicans were actually more concerned that the housework be equitable to both adults. Strong Republicans were 5 percentage points more likely to confess that the division of housework was "unfair to my spouse or partner" than strong Democrats. In marriages it seems the same as in politics: Those on the political left focus on the alleged unfairness to them and do not consider that others might be getting the short end of the stick.[14] Another survey found that feminist women do less housework than traditionalist women, but complain more about it. (Honestly, does this really surprise anyone?)[15]

Liberals are also less satisfied with their marriages. By a 10 percent spread, conservatives are more likely to say they are happy in their marriages. Liberals are nearly twice as likely to say they are "not too happy."[16]

While they are at it, those on the political left are also much more likely to complain about their health than conservatives. The Social Capital Survey found that liberals were more likely to call their health poor or fair, while conservatives were more likely to say it was excellent or very good.[17] Even when you compare liberals and conservatives of the same age and income, in every group, conservatives were more likely to say they were in very good health. So unless one is willing to believe that diseases and infections prefer liberals, there must be something more at work here.

Often overlooked is the fact that self-described liberals are more than three times as likely to have sought out counseling for mental problems than self-described conservatives.[18] Gallup in a scientific survey found Republicans much more likely to report good mental health than Democrats (58 percent to 38 percent). Brack and Zhang, in their research on neuropolitics, found that liberals were 64 percent more likely to suffer from depression, 320 percent (not a typo) more likely to suffer from bipolar disorder, and 50 percent more likely to suffer from mild depression. (Unlike the other studies, however, this was a nonscientific survey.) The same holds true for anxiety disorders. When asked if they ever felt they were going to have a nervous breakdown, 38 percent of liberals said yes compared with only 21 percent of conservatives.[19]

The General Social Survey found similar results. When asked if they had ever had a mental health problem, 30 percent of those who described themselves as extremely liberal said yes, as did 12 percent of liberals. Only 5 percent of those who were very conservative and 6 percent of conservatives said the same. In short, liberals are between two and six times as likely to have had a mental health problem as conservatives. No question that there are medical and biological factors that contribute to depression. Conservatives may also be culturally less disposed to seek psychiatric help when they need it. But the fact remains: The farther to the left you go, the more likely you are to find depression and other related emotional problems.[20]

Mental health problems are no laughing matter. So why do liberals seem to struggle with these issues more than conservatives? Liberals might say that they are simply more self-aware than conservatives. But this seems inadequate to explain the vast disparities documented here. One reason may have to do with the fact that modern liberalism has encouraged extreme individualism and self-focus. Martin Seligman, past president of the American Psychological Association and professor at the University of Pennsylvania, explains that depression is rising in America today for four distinct reasons. All of them have their roots in liberal thought.

First is the problem of what he calls "rampant individualism." "Unipolar depression is a disorder of the thwarting of the 'I,' as we are increasingly taught to view all through the 'I,' " says Seligman. Modern liberalism encourages independence from church, family, and community because they can be suffocating and cramp our individual desires. "Rampant individualism causes us to think that our setbacks are of vast importance and thus something to become depressed about."

The second reason for the rise in depression among liberals is what might be called the self-esteem craze. "Self-esteem emphasis has made millions think there's something fundamentally wrong if you don't feel good, as opposed to just, 'I don't feel good right now, but I will later,' " Seligman explains. (Both of these are prominent features of modern liberalism, as discussed in the chapter "The Mighty Me.")

Another reason for the rise of depression is a pervasive attitude among liberals of "victimology and helplessness." Modern liberalism has created a situation in which pretty much everyone in the country can classify themselves as some sort of victim. This mentality contributes to depression, says Seligman, because it encourages the view that we are passive sufferers who cannot help ourselves.[21] This is certainly the case among liberals, who in surveys regularly claim that they are helpless or that much of what is happening in their lives is beyond their control. "Luck" and "fate" play an outsized role in their lives, and therefore they lack the power to change their circumstances.

The final reason Seligman offers is the growth of modern materialism. Often considered to be a conservative vice, the evidence shows the opposite. Liberals today place much more emphasis on money than conservatives do. (See the chapter above on liberals and money.)

Another reason liberalism leads many into emotional despair is that many of its leading lights have embraced nihilism (i.e., the belief that life has no meaning). Professor Richard Dawkins of Oxford University holds a chair in public understanding of science, but he has a following on the left due to his numerous bestselling books on science, evolution, and religion. Dawkins is regularly featured as a lecturer on college campuses and television. He has appeared on the cover of *Time* magazine and received numerous prestigious awards. A resolute atheist, Dawkins believes that existence "is neither good nor evil, neither kind nor cruel, but simply callous: indifferent to all suffering, lacking all purpose." Jessica Matthews, president of the Carnegie Endowment for International Peace, and former editorial board member and columnist for the *Washington Post,* expressed similar bleak sentiments: "Human life is a cosmic accident with no purpose."[22]

Many popular writers embraced by the left endorse this view. Jean-Paul Sartre viewed all human action as meaningless; novelist Thomas Pynchon pushed the idea that the universe was pointless in critically acclaimed novels such as *Gravity's Rainbow.*[23]

Liberalism has also increasingly embraced an apocalyptic outlook over the past forty years. In the 1950s and '60s, liberals sounded the alarm of economic doom. In 1958, John Kenneth Galbraith wrote in *The Affluent Society* that with a home, a car, a television set, and one person in college, Americans had reached their economic pinnacle. American prosperity could go no higher—and that we ought to be concerned about a political crisis as a result. (A generation later, as Gregg Easterbrook points out, average real income had doubled, entire families were college educated, and several cars were the norm.)

A few years later, Stanford University professor Paul Ehrlich warned that there would be a widespread famine, leading to the deaths of hundreds of millions, and food riots leading to tens of millions more deaths. His book, *Population Bomb,* began, "The battle to feed all of humanity is over . . . hundreds of millions of people are going to starve to death. . . . By 1985 enough millions will have died to reduce the earth's population to some acceptable level, like 1.5 billion people." The same year he cheerily predicted in an article entitled "Eco-Catastrophe!" that the United States would see its life expectancy drop to age forty-two by the year 1980 because of pesticides. By 1999, he warned, the American population would drop to 22.6 million. A few years later he wrote *The End of Affluence,* in which he envisioned the U.S. president dissolving Congress "during the food riots of the 1980s," followed by a nuclear attack resulting from the use of insecticides.[24]

Needless to say, none of what Ehrlich predicted came close to happening. China alone now has about as many people as the 1.5 billion he claimed was all the planet could sustain. Life expectancy is higher than ever. And I must have missed the food riots, unless he's counting the occasional scrum you find at a busy Starbucks. But the left has embraced Ehrlich and his apocalyptic visions to advance an agenda. Ehrlich went on to become a founding father of Earth Day and remains an influential force in the environmental movement. He has been awarded prizes by the World Wildlife Fund, the Sierra Club, the United Nations, and a "genius" award from the MacArthur Foundation.

In 1977, Jimmy Carter warned, "We could use up all of the proven reserves of oil in the entire world by the end of the next decade." In 1980 he formed a special commission that released a report called Global 2000. What would the world be like in the year 2000? Carter's commission envisioned mass starvation all over the developing world, superplagues that would ravage the globe, and the collapse of entire ecosystems. These predictions were embraced by many liberals who prepared themselves for a dark future.

In the 1980s the left embraced another doom-and-gloom scenario: nuclear war and nuclear winter. Terrified by President Reagan's confrontational stance against the Soviet Union, liberals regarded nuclear war as virtually inevitable. Hollywood produced a scare movie, *The Day After,* about a postnuclear-holocaust America. Edward Hume, the film's scriptwriter, explained that he wrote the story because "most people have no sense of the enormity of these weapons and just how suicidal they are." At Brown University, campus radicals pushed a non-binding referendum asking the college to stockpile cyanide pills to facilitate suicide in the event of a nuclear war. Other campuses passed similar measures. The Massachusetts State Health Commission produced television commercials about the evils of a nuclear holocaust. "When I grow up, I want to be alive," a child said in one of these commercials. Dr. Helen Caldicott, an antinuclear activist hailed by many as a hero on the left, told a group of pediatricians: "What is the point of keeping these children alive for another five, ten, or twenty years . . . when during this time they could be vaporized in a nuclear war?"

The late Carl Sagan pushed the idea that nuclear war would send the planet into a long, life-killing artificial winter by blotting out the rays of the sun. This potent fright-scenario remained a siren call for the left until the Soviet Union collapsed. Then they moved on to its virtual opposite, global warming. Today, former vice president Al Gore leads a movement that embraces the language and imagery of the apocalypse. "We are," he claims, "altering the balance of energy between our planet and the rest of the universe."

Gore explains that automobiles are a "mortal threat to the security of every nation that is more deadly than that of any military enemy we are ever again likely to confront." Global warming will not just change temperatures, it will "upset the balance between daylight and darkness." The impact of cutting down tropical rain forests could last for "tens of millions of years." Our heedless attitude toward the environment means we are "making it impossible for our children's children to have a standard of living even remotely similar to ours." Our children face a life in which they will experience "a decade without winter." Given all this, can it be really surprising that Al Gore is depressed? As he writes in his book *Earth in the Balance* (subtitled *Ecology and the Human Spirit*): "The unnatural task of a disembodied mind is to somehow ignore the intense psychic pain that comes from the nagging awareness of what is missing: the experience of living in one's body as a fully integrated physical and mental being." Gore has reported feeling "paralyzed" by his fears of an ecological disaster.[25]

It is entirely possible for someone on the left, over the course of a couple of decades, to have embraced five different visions that would bring about the complete destruction of mankind. In a recent speech at Brown University, lefty billionaire Ted Turner covered all the bases, claiming that "the world is on the brink of collapse" because of "threats of nuclear war, population explosion, and environmental exploitation."[26]

The grim consequence of such apocalyptic thinking is what criminology professor Steve Stack calls an "ideology of suicide." In 1997, six of the most prominent liberal theorists in the United States—Ronald Dworkin, John Rawls, Thomas Nagel, Robert Nozick, Tim Scanlon, and Judith Jarvis Thomson—filed a brief with the Supreme Court declaring that people had a federal constitutional right to physician-assisted suicide.[27] For years the idea of suicide as a rational choice has been pushed by modern liberals. Bill Moyers hosted a four-part PBS series called "On Our Own Terms: Moyers on Dying," in which he encouraged people to "take charge" of life-and-death decisions. Anna Quindlen wrote a book titled *One True Thing,* which showed how taking your own life could be a courageous and rational choice.[28] Much of what the left has to say on suicide stems from what Herbert Marcuse called "the inconvenient reality of death." He believed that "the meaning of death must be changed" and "made rational." Marcuse argued: "After a fulfilled life, they may take it upon themselves to die—at a moment of their own choosing."[29]

This belief system has very real consequences. The fact is, those on the left are much more accepting of suicide—and are correspondingly more likely to attempt it. As Professor Stack puts it, "Political liberalism affects the level of suicide acceptability." Certainly people may commit suicide when plagued with a host of mental illnesses. But many on the modern liberal-left justify suicide as a reasonable course of action. When the General Social Surveys asked if it was okay to commit suicide if you are simply "tired of living," 35 percent of those who were liberal said yes, compared to only 12 percent of conservatives.[30] Liberals also don't seem to have as much of a problem committing suicide if they have "dishonored the family," for example, by getting arrested or otherwise embarrassing their relatives. They are nearly three times as likely to say it's okay to commit suicide in such a circumstance—including 22 percent of those extremely liberal and 15 percent of liberals.[31]

One study by two widely respected academics, Professors Steven Stack and Ira Wasserman, found that liberal social attitudes such as feminism are linked to a "pro-suicide ideology," while conservative attitudes tend to be antisuicide for both blacks and whites.[32] Another study in the academic journal *Sex Roles* found that liberalism is linked with a permissive attitude toward suicide and actual suicide attempts.[33] A 2004 study in the *American Journal of Psychiatry* found that conservative religious people had far fewer suicide attempts than liberals and secular people, even if they had the same levels of depression.[34]

Abbie Hoffman, one of the darlings of the sixties left, committed suicide using 150 pills and a heavy dose of alcohol. According to one of his supporters, Hoffman "saw the unfairness and the meaninglessness of life." Tom Hayden explained his suicide this way: "He was really uncomfortable with becoming middle aged and facing old age without seeing significant social change."[35] New Left leader Paul Krasner saw three of his radical friends commit suicide. His attitude about it is that of many on the left today. "The pain of living was too much for them," he explained in an interview. "It always seemed to me like a waste, but that was their choice."[36]

Many veterans of the sixties left struggled with emotional and psychological problems. Mario Savio, leader of the Berkeley Free Speech Movement, ended up in a mental institution. Robert Starobin, another student leader, committed suicide, as did Marshall Bloom, who helped shut down the London School of Economics. Jerry Rubin ended up joining a cult. Andy Wernick, a Canadian student leader in the 1960s, later recalled that there were a high number of nervous breakdowns among his followers.[37]

Hayden's comment that Hoffman couldn't deal with the fact that society wasn't changing highlights another problem with modern liberalism: Many on the liberal left believe that their individual happiness is contingent on the collective behavior of *other people*. Consider the reactions to recent political elections. The left lost the three national elections between 2000 and 2004. Following each defeat, liberals screamed of rigged elections, unfair practices at the polling booth, and voter intimidation. When George W. Bush won reelection in 2004, Michael Moore was so devastated he couldn't get out of bed for three days. Meanwhile, thousands of liberals flooded Canadian immigration websites inquiring about the possibility of moving north. "I just don't know if I can live here for four more years," one production assistant in Los Angeles complained.[38] Actor Vincent D'Onofrio was reportedly so upset by Bush's victory that he passed out backstage from anxiety.[39]

As Renana Brooks, a clinical psychologist in Washington, D.C., explained in the *Los Angeles Times,* "People are in absolute post-traumatic stress and total despair and pretty much believe American society is permanently destroyed. That's what I've been hearing all day. . . . *It looks to be like a worse trauma than 9/11.*" One Democrat told the paper, "I feel like someone had died." Writer Gene Stone published a *Bush Survival Bible* to help leftists cope with the shattering disappointment. "I was so bummed out by the election so I thought that all that anxiety, depression—all those negative emotions I felt—I thought, hey, I've got a channel to do something about it," the author explained. Stone refers readers to an M.D. who explains how to "fight panic and monitor blood pressure." He also offers "five antidepressants to consider."

Manhattan psychoanalyst Sherman Pheiffer told the Associated Press that many of his liberal patients were in a state of near panic. "My patients are incredulous, depressed, angry, very frightened. . . ." In Palm Beach County, psychotherapist Douglas Schooler treated depressed Democrats through "intense hypnotherapy." "Conservatives are calling me to say these people are weak-kneed kooks, but they're not acknowledging that this is a normal psychological response to a severe and disillusioning situation," he explained.

In 2003, John Kerry complained that he was unfairly maligned by the Swift Boat Veterans for Truth and filed a lawsuit—the first ever against a political campaign ad by a presidential candidate. Six months after his defeat, Kerry traveled across the country whining about the loss. People were denied access to the polls through trickery and intimidation, he told the League of Women Voters. "Leaflets are handed out saying Democrats vote on Wednesday, Republicans vote on Tuesday," he said. "People are told in telephone calls that if you've ever had a parking ticket, you're not allowed to vote." A lawsuit was filed in Ohio (it was dismissed by the Ohio Supreme Court). Kerry never presented a shred of evidence for his charges. But he was convinced of one thing: He was a victim.

No one likes to lose, but Richard Nixon never challenged his narrow loss to John F. Kennedy in 1960, even though there were widespread credible reports of ballot tampering in Chicago. Can anyone recall George H. W. Bush grousing about how Ross Perot cost him the White House in 1992? Were there cries of vote rigging and manipulative tactics when Bill Clinton won reelection in 1996, or when Republicans lost the '06 congressional elections? Does anyone recall conservatives like Sean Hannity lying in bed for three days after Clinton was reelected? Did George W. Bush file a lawsuit against Michael Moore for his unfair portrayal in *Fahrenheit 9/11*? Of course not. To be sure, conservatives responded with disappointment. But they moved on and didn't wallow in despondency.

Garrison Keillor was in San Francisco when the 2004 results came in. He said he experienced "exquisite pain." "It's true what our parents told us," he said. "It only takes one person to mess things up for everybody." Many on the left agree with Keillor: One person can wreck everything for everyone. In other words, liberals tend to be dependent on the behavior of others to maintain their own happiness.

The singer Linda Ronstadt, an outspoken liberal, explained the emotional challenges she faces just being near conservatives. "It's a real conflict for me when I go to a concert and find out somebody in the audience is a Republican or fundamental Christian," she explains. "It can cloud my enjoyment. I'd rather not know."[40] Can you imagine a conservative saying such a boorish thing? Yet liberals are the ones who pride themselves on being tolerant and open-minded.

Sometimes our liberal friends seek to create a sense of being victimized or threatened where none exists. When Garrison Keillor was invited to speak at the Highland Park United Methodist Church, more than a thousand people showed up to listen to him and asked him to sign copies of his book *Homegrown Democrat*. The speech seemed to go exceedingly well, and newspaper accounts reported that he was interrupted with applause from his fans. Days later, however, he wrote a *Chicago Tribune* article that painted a dark image of the event. Keillor, it turns out, had been the victim of intimidation and hostility. "I got some insight last week into who supports torture when I went down to Dallas to speak at Highland Park Methodist Church. It was spooky." Keillor explained that he was "met by two burly security men" before the event and felt threatened. The crowd was hostile, he claimed. Several audience members apparently sought to intimidate him in advance of his speech with hints that the Bushes had attended the church.

Keillor's account stunned the event's organizers and attendees. Those "burly security guards" were only present because *Keillor had requested them* through his publisher. And his publicist admitted that he had had no contact with any church or audience members prior to the speech. Those who attended the event simply had no idea what he was talking about. "He was very well received," one fan told the *Dallas Morning News*. "The crowd adored him, laughing and applauding throughout the hour." The minister who invited Keillor to speak, Rev. Paul Rasmussen, was equally stunned. "It's unsettling," he said. "We felt like we had a very successful event. You read this article and think, 'Hey, what happened?'" [41]

One reason for the left's tendency to whine and complain is that modern liberalism has eschewed personal accountability and embraced collective indictment. The great exception to this liberal axiom, of course, is that it doesn't apply to conservatives. In that event, the individual is responsible for a multiplicity of sins. Consider this from Keillor, explaining how George W. Bush is responsible for drinking on college campuses. "Children have lost hope of achieving the good life their parents and grandparents have; they expect to slide into debt to pay for a mediocre education, get a minimum-wage job, live in Mom's basement, and slide into their thirties. No wonder they're depressed and resort to alcohol and devastating drugs. 'You going to party?' they say, and for them party means 'drink until unconscious.' When I walk past college bars at night and see beautiful young women vomiting between parked cars, I wish Mr. Bush were there to hold their heads."[42]

Say again?

Many liberals believe that society at large is responsible for the security, health, and happiness of individuals. Conservatives believe that individuals are responsible for themselves. This difference explains why 34 percent of liberals said in one survey that the problems of life were just too big to cope with, while only 19 percent of conservatives agreed. Liberals often feel overwhelmed by life's problems because they are waiting for the government to fix them. When it doesn't, liberals blame others (and "society") for their misfortune.

The disaster of Hurricane Katrina in 2005 offers an interesting counterpoint. Liberal New Orleans and conservative Mississippi were both devastated by the storm. The damage across the region was enormous; some even concluded that the Mississippi coast suffered more than the Crescent City. But the response by people in those two areas was vastly different.

In New Orleans there was a wholesale embrace of the culture of complaint. Even before the winds died down, Gov. Kathleen Blanco and Mayor Ray Nagin began pointing fingers, blaming the federal government, state government,

Army Corps of Engineers, the people who oversaw the levees, the U.S. Army and National Guard, and FEMA. There were plenty of press conferences and television interviews. Governor Blanco even danced with the displaced in the New Orleans Superdome as a "sign of solidarity." The cleanup began, but at a glacial pace. When complaints arose that the cleanup was going too slow, Nagin pointed to the fact that the World Trade Center had not yet been rebuilt. When criticized for sending city workers to Las Vegas and Atlantic City just weeks after the disaster, Nagin again played the victim. "You've got to understand," he said. "New Orleans is a party town."[43]

A Katrina National Justice Commission was formed, to determine what role racism and oppression played in the disaster. Sponsored by the NAACP and a variety of civil rights organizations, the commission was assembled to "hear stories of people's Katrina struggle." Hearings were held for two days in the ballroom of the Sheraton Hotel. (The proceedings were interrupted by eighty-three-year-old black restaurateur Leah Chase, who snapped, "You can't blame anyone; you've just got to move on. . . . If you only do what you're supposed to do, you'll overcome all this. You have to stop whining and move on." Alas, her suggestion was ignored.)[44]

Then Jesse Jackson showed up. Not to assist with the cleanup and rebuilding, mind you, but to protest. Along with Mayor Ray Nagin, Congressman William Jefferson, and Sheila Jackson-Lee, Jackson and his cohorts from the Rainbow Coalition marched down the streets of the Ninth Ward demanding more assistance. Four other Jackson visits were spent protesting, not rebuilding.[45]

Meanwhile, in Mississippi the disaster has been handled in a completely different fashion. Although suffering more damage over a wider area, the cleanup and rebuilding started immediately and is much further advanced than in New Orleans. When asked how the state was doing, Gov. Haley Barbour responded: "We're not into whining, moping, and we're not into victimhood in Mississippi." Barbour said, "Our people got up, hitched up their britches, and went to work helping themselves and helping their neighbors."

With all the whining, complaining, and lack of progress in New Orleans, the plight of Mississippi has been largely forgotten. "I've noticed that the news media chose to cover New Orleans long before Mississippi was viewed as going in the right direction," Barbour sagely observed. "You know, the news media doesn't like to cover airplanes that land safely. I think the good stories about Mississippi are not as newsworthy in people's minds."[46]

Conservatives certainly believe that injustices exist and that bad things can happen to good people. But they choose to handle such misfortunes differently. Booker T. Washington expressed the antidote to the victim culture decades ago when he proclaimed that moral worth was not determined by how much one has been victimized, but by what one does to overcome one's victimhood. More recently Thomas Sowell captured this spirit succinctly when he explained: "Victimhood is something to escape, not something to exploit."

CONCLUSION
Why Did I Write This Book?

I began this book with two simple assumptions: first, that ideas influence our behavior; and second, that modern liberals and conservatives have distinctly different behavioral patterns reflecting their different philosophies. Liberal academics, often using strange methodologies, ideologically slanted "observations," or theories created from whole cloth, have argued that conservatives are plagued by a multitude of character flaws. Many conservatives, on the other hand, have argued that liberal ideas have a damaging influence on our society. Our coarsening culture, a growing sense of entitlement, an inordinate focus on self, and other elements of modern liberalism have caused or contributed to the unraveling of the American social fabric and the decline of the American character.

Up until now, no one has marshaled the evidence to demonstrate where the truth actually lies. That is also why so much of the debate on this question has been so shrill and angry: precisely because it has been a fight over opinion rather than facts. The evidence presented here clearly shows not only that modern liberalism damages the social fabric, but that it has also had a deleterious effect on individuals. Liberal ideas do have consequences for those who embrace them—and for the rest of us as well.

This is partly what makes liberalism so appealing: It is a philosophy of lip service to virtuous ideals that demands little if any action from its adherents. As a proponent of liberal ideals, one is free to focus on one's rights and totally neglect one's responsibilities; actual charity for the less fortunate involving personal sacrifice is replaced by simply supporting governmental programs (and the liberal candidates who espouse them); truth is relative, so honesty and the aggressive pursuit of truth make little sense; victimhood is embraced, and complaining about one's personal difficulties (real or imagined) becomes a noble act; displaying one's anger is a sign of "authenticity" and "concern"; embracing liberal beliefs is a sign of superior intelligence, and therefore actually being informed seems to matter less; simply denouncing our "moneymaking culture" makes you morally pure and therefore frees you to pursue wealth all the more aggressively; the free market system is rigged, so hard work is not a virtue, and a free-riding attitude is tacitly encouraged.

This is not what liberalism used to be. The classical liberalism of Locke, Madison, and Mill did offer instruction on virtue and spoke of the obligations that individuals possessed in addition to their rights. But all that dramatically changed with the sixties ethos of personal liberation, which transformed liberalism into something completely different.

Today's liberalism would be hardly recognizable to the liberals of the past. Tocqueville famously praised the American people for their self-reliance. Jefferson and the other founding fathers saw the damaging influence that servile dependency on a monarch could have on the American character. Harry Truman would have had little patience for the victim culture. He understood that victims existed, but wanted to exalt them for rising up, not wallowing in self-pity. Woodrow Wilson would have been deeply troubled by the self-absorption of modern liberalism. Wilson believed that we have obligations and responsibilities that go beyond simply supporting a government program. Franklin Delano Roosevelt was many things, but it is unlikely that he would have been comfortable with the collective whining that passes for liberal activism today. John F. Kennedy (for all his flaws) would not have embraced envy as a virtue, or an accurate measure of what is just.

When conservatives talk about cultivating virtue—hard work, honesty, family, charity—it is not a wedge issue trotted out for campaigns. It is actually a reflection of what conservatism means, and what conservatives value. Virtue is vital for the moral health of individuals and for the survival of our society. As Professor Peter Berkowitz puts it: "All political societies depend on the practice of virtue and the preservation of core values, but perhaps none more so than a liberal democracy, where equality in freedom enables individuals to live by their own lights and gives them large scope for making bad choices and indulging silly or false opinions."[1]

So why did I write this book? Partly, of course, to demonstrate the truth and value of my own position as an avowed conservative. To that extent, I doubt that many liberals will be persuaded by this book to abandon their political ideas. But it is also my hope that by exposing the true nature of the link between ideas and behavior, the book may serve to put the era of ad hominem politics behind us. To date, the argument about the difference between conservatives and liberals has been dominated by opinion and invective. This has been as true on the right as it has on the left. With the weight of evidence now clear, maybe liberals will give up attacking conservatives for what are really their own sins, and we can begin to focus once again on the merits of people's ideas, rather than their failings as individuals.

Maybe. But I'm not holding my breath.

NOTES

INTRODUCTION

1. George Lakoff, *Moral Politics* (Chicago: University of Chicago Press, 2002), pp. xv and 391.

2. Kurt Kleiner, "How to Spot a Baby Conservative," *Chicago Sun-Times,* March 19, 2006.

3. "Researchers Help Define What Makes a Political Conservative," *UCBerkeley News,* July 22, 2003.

4. Quoted in William Martin, *The Best Liberal Quotes Ever: Why the Left Is Right* (Naperville, IL: Sourcebooks, 2004), p. 41.

5. Karen Stenner, *The Authoritarian Dynamic* (New York: Cambridge University Press, 2005).

6. Joel Bleifuss, "Conservatives Deconstructed," *In These Times,* October 2003.

7. American Council of Trustees and Alumni, "Intellectual Diversity," December 2005.

8. Robert Kuttner, "The Politics of Family," *American Prospect,* April 8, 2002.

9. Anne-Marie O'Connor, *Los Angeles Times,* October 26, 2005.

10. Garrison Keillor, "We're Not in Lake Wobegon Anymore," *In These Times,* August 27, 2004.

11. Brian C. Anderson, "Illiberal Liberalism," *City Journal* (spring 2001).

12. William O'Rourke, "Bush's Yahoo Nation," *Chicago Sun-Times,* November 14, 2000.

13. Quoted in J. Peder Zane, "Is Dubya Really That Dumb?" *News and Observer,* January 24, 2001.

14. Kurt Vonnegut, "Strange Weather Lately," *In These Times,* May 9, 2003.

15. Jane Smiley, "The Unteachable Ignorance of the Red States," Slate.com, November 4, 2004.

16. Herbert McClosky, "Conservatism and Personality," *American Political Science Review* (March 1957).

17. William D. McIntosh, Rebecca M. Murray, John D. Murray, and Debra Sabia, "Are the Liberal Good in Hollywood?: Characteristics of Political Figures in Popular Films from 1945 to 1998," *Communication Reports,* vol. 16, no. 1 (2003).

18. Robert L. Bartley, "Angry Democrats: Lost Birthright," *Wall Street Journal,* September 22, 2003.

19. Andrew Ferguson, "*New York* Magazine's Doctors Analyze Bush," Bloomberg News, February 13, 2007.

20. James Piereson, *Camelot and the Cultural Revolution* (New York: Encounter Books, 2007).

21. Ted Rall, "Win or Lose, Kerry Voters Are Smarter Than Bush Voters," *San Antonio Express,* November 9, 2004.

22. Brian C. Anderson, "Illiberal Liberalism," *City Journal* (spring 2001).

23. See Jim Rutenberg, "Campaigns Use TV Preferences to Find Voters," *New York Times,* July 18, 2004, and John Tierney, "Your Car: Politics on Wheels," *New York Times,* April 1, 2005.

24. See Bruce Fleming, *Why Liberals and Conservatives Clash* (New York: Routledge, 2006).

25. "Religion and the Public Square: Attitudes of American Jews in Comparative Perspective," Special Report, Jerusalem Center for Public Affairs, August 1, 2000.

26. For a summation of the research in this area, see Satoshi Kanazawa, "Who Lies on Surveys, and What Can We Do About It?" *Journal of Social, Political and Economic Studies,* vol. 30, no. 3 (fall 2005).

1. Peter Carlson, "Yakety Facts: The Word on Clinton in *Vanity Fair,*" *Washington Post,* May 18, 2004.

2. General Social Survey, Cumulative Datafile.

3. See Arthur C. Brooks, "The Fertility Gap," *Wall Street Journal,* August 22, 2006.

4. Ilene Lilchuk, "Barking Up the Same Old Tree," *San Francisco Chronicle,* July 6, 2005, and Phillip Longman, "The Liberal Baby Bust," *USA Today,* March 13, 2006.

5. Joel Kotkin, "We Don't Need a Cool Mayor," *Los Angeles Times,* May 9, 2005.

6. Cheryle Wetzstein, "More American Women Pull Plugs on Biological Clocks," *Washington Times,* November 22, 2000.

7. Ken Auletta, "The Lost Tycoon," *New Yorker,* April 23, 2001.

8. World Values Survey, Cumulative Datafile. Since ideology is placed on a scale from 1 to 10 (1 very liberal, 10 very conservative), I am using responses from categories 1 to 3 and 8 to 10.

9. Conversation on yelp.com.

10. Thedailypage.com/forum/viewtopic.php?t=17983& view=next.

11. "Where Have All the Flower Children Gone?" *Florida Sun-Sentinel,* October 10, 1998.

12. http://www.yelp.com/topic/cEsiD2AeeOt3dJhe6 EEJ_g.

13. Happyfeminist.typepad.com.

14. General Social Survey, Cumulative Datafile.

15. For a good summation, see Laura Tennant, "Marriage Has Been Tragically Unfashionable Among the Left-Leaning Classes Since the 1970s—But What If It's Actually Our Best Chance of Happiness?" *New Statesman,* March 27, 2006.

16. Barbara Ehrenreich, "Oh, Those Family Values," *Time,* June 24, 2001, and "Will Women Still Need Men?" *Time,* February 21, 2000.

17. Catharine MacKinnon, *Feminism Unmodified: Discourses on Life and Law* (Cambridge: Harvard University Press, 1987).

18. Linda Hirshman, "Homeward Bound," *Salon,* November 21, 2005.

19. Quoted in Valerie Polakow, *The Erosion of Childhood* (Chicago: University of Chicago Press, 1992).

20. Gloria Steinem, *Revolution from Within: A Book of Self-Esteem* (Boston: Little, Brown, 1993).

21. Adrianne Frost, *I Hate Other People's Kids* (New York: Simon Spotlight Entertainment, 2006), and Jason DeParle, "The Case Against Kids: When Parents Sacrifice Their Ideals in the Name of Their Children, Both Suffer," *Washington Monthly* (July–August 1988).

22. Nancy Romen, "Childless: Some by Chance, Some by Choice," *Washington Post,* November 28, 2006.

23. Sarah Klein, "Oh (No) Baby," *Detroit Metro Times,* January 10, 2006.

24. Christopher Clausen, "Childfree in Toyland," *American Scholar* (winter 2002).

25. See Hirshman, "Homeward Bound," and her book *Get to Work: A Manifesto for Women of the World* (New York: Viking, 2006).

26. www.gatago.com/alt/abortion/13590892.html.

27. This story was relayed to me by Professor Paul Kengor.

28. Quoted in Brian C. Anderson, "Illiberal Liberalism," *City Journal* (spring 2001).

29. See Robert S. Lichter and Stanley Rothman, "The Radical Personality: Social Psychology Components of New Left Ideology," *Political Behavior,* vol. 4, no. 3 (1982). See also Lichter and Rothman, "Jewish Ethnicity and Radical Culture: A Social Psychology Study of Political Activists," *Political Psychology,* vol. 3, no. ½ (1981–82).

30. P. J. Watson, Ralph W. Wood, Shelley G. Foster, and Ronald J. Mears, "Sin, Depression, and Narcissism," *Review of Religious Research,* vol. 29, no. 3 (1988).

31. World Values Survey, Cumulative Datafile.

32. National Cultural Values Survey, Culture and Media Institute, Special Report, 2007.

33. General Social Survey, Cumulative Datafile.

34. "Security Check," *The Economist,* May 17, 2007.

35. National Cultural Values Survey, see note 32.

36. World Values Survey, Cumulative Datafile.

37. John P. Bartowski and W. Bradford Wilcox, "Conservative Child Discipline: The Case of Parental Yelling," *Social Forces,* vol. 79, no. 1 (September 2000): 265–90.

38. W. Bradford Wilcox, "Religion, Convention and Paternal Involvement," *Journal of Marriage and the Family,* vol. 64 (2002): 780–92.

39. Laura Fingerson, "Do Mothers' Opinions Matter in Teens' Sexual Activity?" *Journal of Family Issues,* vol. 26 (October 2005): 947–74.

40. Rachel K. Jones, Jacqueline E. Darroch, and Sushella Singh, "Religious Differentials in the Sexual and Reproductive Behaviors of Young Women in the United States," *Journal of Adolescent Health,* vol. 36 (2005): 279–88.

41. General Social Survey, Cumulative Datafile.

42. Quoted in Harry Stein, *How I Accidentally Joined the Vast Right Wing Conspiracy (and Found Inner Peace)* (New York: Delacorte Press, 2000).

43. General Social Survey, Cumulative Datafile.

44. Daniel P. Moals and Christopher Ellison, "Who Buys New Age Materials? Exploring Sociodemographic, Religious, Network, and Contextual Correlations of New Age Consumption," *Sociology of Religion* (fall 2000);

Michael J. Donahue, "Prevalence and Correlates of New Age Beliefs in Six Protestant Denominations," *Journal for the Scientific Study of Religion,* vol. 32, no. 2 (1993); and Wendy Kaminer, *Sleeping with Extra-Terrestrials: The Rise of Irrationalism and Perils of Piety* (New York: Vintage, 1999).

45. Quoted in Tom Corwin, "Drugs: Public Could Ignore Issue," *Augusta Chronicle,* July 28, 1996.

46. Bonnie Erbe, *Rocky Mountain News,* August 24, 1999.

47. *American Morning,* CNN transcript, December 19, 2006.

48. Franken, quoted in *Dallas Morning News,* October 5, 2002.

49. Douglas Brinkley, "Football Season Is Over," *Rolling Stone,* September 8, 2005.

50. "The Truth About Hunter S. Thompson," CNN.com, October 12, 2007.

51. Katherine Q. Seelye, "Ashes to Fireworks Send-Off for an 'Outlaw' Writer," *New York Times*, August 22, 2005.

52. Quoted in Dick Williams, "The Legacy of Abbie Hoffman: An America That's Ravaged by Drugs," *Atlanta Journal-Constitution,* April 22, 1989.

53. Bill McAllister, "Reagan Derides Critics of His Antidrug Policies," *Washington Post,* September 10, 1988, and Godfrey Sperling, "Liberal Intellectuals Out of Step on Drugs," *Christian Science Monitor,* April 4, 1989.

54. "Under the Clintons, the Drug Hemorrhage Has Gotten Worse," *Richmond Times-Dispatch,* October 3, 1996.

55. Richard Blum et al., *Students and Drugs* (San Francisco: Jossey-Bass, 1969).

56. Michael Newcomb and Tamra Burns Loeb, "Poor Parenting as an Adult Problem Behavior: General Deviance, Deviant Attitudes, Inadequate Family Support and Bonding, or Just Bad Parents?" *Journal of Family Psychology* (June 1999).

57. Ibid.

58. Michael S. Dunn, "The Relationship Between Religiosity, Employment, and Political Beliefs on Substance Use among High School Seniors," *Journal of Alcohol and Drug Education* (March 2005).

59. General Social Survey, Cumulative Datafile.

60. Charles T. Tart, *On Being Stoned: A Psychological Study of Marijuana Intoxication* (Palo Alto: Science and Behavior Books, 1971), and Erich Goode, *The Marijuana Smokers* (New York: Basic Books, 1970).

61. Robert Trevino, "Attitudes Toward Drug Legalization Among Drug Users," *American Journal of Drug and Alcohol Abuse* (February 2002).

62. Satoshi Kanazawa, "Who Lies on Surveys, and What Can We Do About It?" *Journal of Social, Political and Economic Studies,* vol. 30, no. 3 (fall 2005).

CHAPTER 2

1. Michael Levin, "How Do People's Politics Affect Their Giving?" *Nonprofit World* (January–February 1999).

2. *New York Times,* July 1, 2003.

3. Hillary Clinton, *Living History* (New York: Simon & Schuster, 2003).

4. Garrison Keillor, *Homegrown Democrat: A Few Plain Thoughts from the Heart of America* (New York: Penguin, 2006).

5. Mark Adomanis, "No Conspiracy Here," *Harvard Crimson,* April 29, 2004.

6. E-mail correspondence with Professor Arthur Brooks, October 29, 2007.

7. Leslie Eaton, "Cuomo Is Richest of Major-Party Candidates," *New York Times,* May 11, 2002. The website is andrewcuomo.com.

8. Eaton, "Cuomo Is Richest."

9. Al Gore, "Remarks by Vice President Al Gore to the DLC 1998 Annual Conference," December 2, 1998, available at DLC.org.

10. "Gores' Charitable Giving Raises Some Eyebrows," CNN.com, April 15, 1998.

11. Ibid.

12. Gore, "Remarks by Vice President Al Gore."

13. Byron York, "John Kerry's Bright Financial Picture," *National Review Online,* April 14, 2004.

14. Al Hunt, "Politics and People," *Wall Street Journal*, February 19, 1998.

15. "The Kennedy 1040," *Time*, June 3, 1974.

16. Robert Reich, *Reason: Why Liberals Will Win the Battle for America* (New York: Vintage, 2005), pp. 55, 116.

17. Stephanie Ebbert, "Reich Made $1 Million in 2001," *Boston Globe*, April 17, 2002.

18. Jennifer Medina, "Lieberman's Challenger Releases Tax Return for Last Year," *New York Times*, July 22, 2006.

19. See Reagan's publicly released tax returns, 1980–89.

20. Dennis Conrad, "Obama's Income Put at $991,296," Associated Press, April 16, 2007.

21. "Pelosi: Census Report Shows Republicans Have Turned Deaf Ear to Middle Class and Working Families," U.S. Newswire, August 30, 2005.

22. "Pelosi: Not Only Is Republican Budget Fiscally Reckless and Dishonest, It Is Morally Irresponsible," States News Service, March 17, 2005.

23. "Pelosi: It Is an Act of Worship to Minister to Needs of World's Poorest," States News Service, January 18, 2005.

24. All of this information comes from the 990 tax forms that these individuals file with the Internal Revenue Service.

25. Barbra Streisand Foundation, 990PF form, filed with the IRS.

26. See Michael Moore's 990PF tax forms for the years 2000–2005.

27. Keillor, *Homegrown Democrat,* p. 184.

28. 990PF tax filings on record with the IRS.

29. Stanley Rothman and Amy Blair, "Media and Business Elites: Still in Conflict," *Public Interest* (spring 2001).

30. General Social Survey, Cumulative Datafile.

31. Arthur C. Brooks, *Who Really Cares?* (New York: Basic Books, 2006).

32. Barna Group Survey of 1,003 people, October 2006.

33. General Social Survey, Cumulative Datafile.

34. National Youth Survey, 2004 variables q6 for "volunteer" and q76 for "ideology."

35. Fred Fessenden, "Jackson Aide Hedges on Income Issue," *Newsday,* May 5, 1988.

36. 990PF form of the Jackson Foundation, IRS, 2004.

37. Erin O'Donnell, "Twigs Bent Left or Right," *Harvard,* January–February 2006.

38. Mark Sappenfield, "Homeless Haven Rethinks Tolerance," *Christian Science Monitor,* March 5, 2002.

39. "NorCal Goats Herd Away Homeless in San Francisco," KNBC.com.

40. The Social Capital Community Benchmark Survey, Cumulative Datafile.

41. Bruce Fleming, *Why Liberals and Conservatives Clash* (New York: Routledge, 2006).

42. Ibid.

43. James T. Lindgren, "Testing Social Dominance: Is Support for Capitalism and Opposition to Income Redistribution Driven by Racism and Intolerance?" *Northwestern Law and Economics Research Paper,* no. 06-10.

44. Ian Simpson Ross, *The Life of Adam Smith* (Oxford: Clarendon Press, 1995).

CHAPTER 3

1. Todd Purdum, "Hillary Clinton Finding a New Voice," *New York Times,* March 30, 1995.

2. John Solomon and Matt Mosk, "For Clinton, New Wealth in Speeches," *Washington Post,* February 23, 2007.

3. Gerald Carbone, "Turner Urges Students to Save the World," *Providence Journal,* February 12, 2002.

4. Jay Nordlinger, "Rosie O'Donnell, Political Activist," *National Review,* June 19, 2000.

5. Sean Wilentz, "Money for Nothing," *New Republic,* February 9, 1998.

6. Bill Clinton, post–State of the Union speech in Buffalo, New York, January 20, 1999.

7. Jim Weaver, *Two Kinds: The Genetic Origin of Conservatives and Liberals* (London: Baird, 1992).

8. "The Liberal Professors," *Eugene, Oregon Register-Guard,* April 7, 2005.

9. Al Kamen, "Those Greedy Sloth-Like Liberals," *Washington Post,* December 4, 1995.

10. General Social Survey, Cumulative Datafile.

11. World Values Survey, Cumulative Datafile.

12. Michael Moore, *Dude, Where's My Country?* (New York: Warner Books, 2003).

13. Jacques Benninga and Edward Wynne, "Keeping in Character," *Phi Delta Kappan,* vol. 79, no. 6 (1998).

14. Nicholas von Hoffman, "Kerry's Not to Blame for America's Delusions," *New York Observer,* September 27, 2004.

15. Quoted in George Gilder, *Wealth and Poverty* (San Francisco: ICS Press, 1993), p. 11.

16. Eileen Buris, "When Work Is Slavery," *Social Justice,* vol. 25 (1998).

17. The Barna Group, national survey conducted October 2006, of 1,003 adults. Data courtesy of the Barna Group.

18. Diane Keyser Wentworth, Robert M. Chell, "College Students and the Protestant Work Ethic," *Journal of Social Psychology* (June 1997).

19. Thomas Li-Ping Tang and Jen Yann Tzeng, "Some Demographic Correlates of the Protestant Work Ethic," April 1988, Education Resources Information Center (ERIC), U.S. Department of Education, # ED300702; Adrian Furnham and Eva Koritsas, "The Protestant

Work Ethic and Vocational Preference," *Journal of Organizational Behavior,* vol. 11, no. 43–45 (1990); Adrian Furnham, "The PWE, Voting Behavior and Attitudes Towards Unions," *Political Studies,* vol. 32, no. 3: 420–36; and Bruce Kirkcaldy, Rudiger Trimpop, Corinna Fischer, and Adrian Furnham, "Leisure and Work Beliefs of British Senior Managers," *Journal of Management Development,* vol. 16, no. 6 (1997).

20. Furnham and Koritsas, "Protestant Work Ethic."

21. Alan M. Saks, "Relationship Between Work Ethic, Job Attitude, Intentions to Quit, and Turnover for Temporary Service Employees," *Revue Canadienne des Sciences de l'Administration* (September 1996); R. G. Poulton and S. H. Ng, "Relationship Between Protestant Work Ethic and Work Effort in a Field Setting," *Applied Psychology: An International Review,* no. 37: 227–33; and R. Eisenberger and D. M. Shank, "Personal Work Ethic and Effort Training Affect Cheating," *Journal of Personality and Social Psychology,* no. 49: 520–28.

22. Lewis S. Feuer, "Some Irrational Sources of Opposition to the Market System," in Ernest van den Haag, ed., *Capitalism: Sources of Hostility* (New Rochelle, NY: Epoch Books, 1979), pp. 109–10.

23. Kirkcaldy et al., "Leisure and Work Beliefs."

24. General Social Survey, Cumulative Datafile.

25. Ibid.

26. Linda J. Skitka and Philip E. Tetlock, "Providing Public Assistance: Cognitive and Motivational Processes Underlying Liberal and Conservative Policy Preferences," *Journal of Personality and Social Psychology* (December 1993).

27. Daniel John Zizzo and Andrew Oswald, "Are People Willing to Pay to Reduce Others' Incomes?" July 2, 2001; and Daniel John Zizzo, "Money Burning and Stealing in the Laboratory: How Conflicting Ideologies Emerge," Department of Economics Discussion Papers Series, Oxford University, no. 40 (October 2000).

28. Ralph Reiland, "When Greed Keeps People in Their Places," *Insight on the News,* September 27, 1999.

29. Adrian Furnham, "Many Sides of the Coin: The Psychology of Money Usage," *Personality and Individual Differences,* no. 5 (1984).

30. James Lindberg, "Testing Social Dominance: Is Support for Capitalism and Opposition to Income Redistribution Driven by Racism and Intolerance?" *Northwestern Law and Economics Research Paper,* no. 06-10.

31. Helmut Schoeck, *Envy: A Theory of Social Behavior* (Indianapolis: Liberty Fund, 1987), p. 128.

32. Quoted in ibid.

33. John Kekes, "Dangerous Egalitarian Dreams," *City Journal* (autumn 2001).

CHAPTER 4

1. Allan Bloom, *The Closing of the American Mind* (New York: Simon & Schuster, 1987).

2. Quoted in Ralph Keyes, *The Post-Truth Era: Dishonesty and Deception in Contemporary Life* (New York: St. Martin's Press, 2004).

3. World Values Survey, Cumulative Datafile.

4. Ibid.

5. National Cultural Values Survey, Culture and Media Institute, Special Report, 2006.

6. Joshua Muravchik, "The Mind of George Soros," *Commentary Magazine,* March 2004.

7. World Values Survey, Cumulative Datafile.

8. *Sex, Drugs, and the 1040: A Barometer of Modern Morals,* Pew Research Center, March 28, 2006.

9. Fred Kaplan, *Gore Vidal: A Biography* (New York: Anchor Books, 2000).

10. Hughlene Burton, Stewart Karlinsky, Cindy Blanthorne, "Perceptions of White Collar Crime: Tax Evasion," May 2005 Working Paper Series, Curtin Business School, Curtin University (Australia), p. 5, also published in *American Taxation Association Journal of Legal Tax Research,* vol. 3. (2005).

11. Mohammed Y. A. Rawwas and Hans K. Isakson, "Ethics of Tomorrow's Business Managers: The Influence of Personal Beliefs and Values, Individual Characteristics,

and Situational Factors," *Journal of Education for Business* (July–August 2000).

12. Jennifer L. Nevins, William O. Bearden, Bruce Money, "Ethical Values and Long-Term Orientation," *Journal of Business Ethics,* no. 71 (2007). See also E. J. Kennedy and L. Lanton, "Religiousness and Business Ethics," *Journal of Business Ethics,* vol. 17, no. 2 (1998): 163–76.

13. World Values Survey, Cumulative Datafile.

14. Scott Vitell, Joseph G. P. Paolillo, and Jatinder J. Singh, "The Role of Money and Religiosity in Determining Consumers' Ethical Beliefs," *Journal of Business Ethics,* vol. 64, no. 2 (2006).

15. World Values Survey, Cumulative Datafile.

16. The Barna Group Survey, October 2006.

17. Roger C. Katz, Jennifer Santman, and Pamela Lonero, "Findings on the Revised Morally Debatable Behaviors Scale," *Journal of Psychology,* vol. 128, no. 1 (1994).

18. Vitell, Paolillo, and Singh, "The Role of Money."

19. National Cultural Values Survey, Culture and Media Institute, Special Report, 2006.

20. Dean Alkmon, Diana Page, and Ralph Roberts, "Determinants of Perceptions of Cheating," *Journal of Business Ethics* (fall 2000).

21. Sal Marino, "People Who Cheat at Golf Cheat in Business," *Industry Week,* October 5, 1998.

22. Dwight Perry, "That's One Way to Be Par for the Course," *Seattle Times,* May 31, 2006.

23. General Social Survey, Cumulative Datafile.

24. Brenda Cossman, "The New Politics of Adultery," *Columbia Journal of Gender and Law* (2006).

25. Bill Dedman, "Reading Hillary Clinton," MSNBC, March 3, 2007, and Ryan Lizza, "The Agitator," *New Republic,* March 9, 2007.

26. Saul Alinsky, *Rules for Radicals: A Practical Primer for Realistic Radicals* (New York: Random House, 1971).

27. Ibid.

28. Hillary Clinton, *Living History* (New York: Simon & Schuster, 2003).

29. These examples are taken from Keyes, *Post-Truth Era.*

30. Derek Harper, "Atlantic City Mayor Levy Admits He Was Never Green Beret," *Press of Atlantic City,* November 10, 2006.

31. Alan Anderson, "GOP Road to White House Could Be Paved with Lies," *Insight on the News,* February 2, 1998.

32. Quoted in Keyes, *Post-Truth Era.*

33. "I Thought I Would Get Away with It. I Knew It Was Nuts," *Daily Mirror,* June 24, 2004.

34. Quoted in Jonah Goldberg, "A Clinton Advocate," *National Review Online,* October 20, 2000.

35. Stephen Goode and Timothy Maier, "Adultery in Public Office," *Insight on the News,* March 2, 1998.

36. 1996 American National Election Study, with variables v961112 ("Post trait: Clinton-moral") and v961269 ("Respondents self-placement on a liberal-conservative 7 point scale").

37. Harry Stein, *How I Accidentally Joined the Vast Right Wing Conspiracy* (New York: Delacorte Press, 2000), p. 31.

38. The details here are from Francis Wheen, *Idiot Proof* (New York: Public Affairs, 2004).

39. Oliver Stone, presentation to Nation Institute panel on "Hollywood and History: The Debate over JFK," March 3, 1992.

40. Richard W. White Jr., *Rude Awakenings: What the Homeless Crisis Tells Us* (San Francisco: ICS Press, 1992).

41. Stanley Diamond, "Reversing Brawley," *The Nation,* October 31, 1988.

42. Edward Jay Epstein, *News from Nowhere* (New York: Random House, 1974).

43. F. G. Bailey, *The Prevalence of Deceit* (Ithaca, NY: Cornell University Press, 1991).

44. Thomas Bender, " 'Facts' and History," *Radical History Review* (March 1985).

45. Ellen Somekawa and Elizabeth A. Smith, "Theorizing the Writing of History or 'I Can't Think Why It Should

Be So Dull, for a Great Deal of It Must Be Invention,' "
Journal of Social History (fall 1988).

46. Lindsay Waters, "Is Now the Time for Paul de Man?" Address to members of the Modern Language Association on the twentieth anniversary of Paul de Man's death.

47. Barbara Johnson, quoted in David Lehman, *Signs of the Times: Deconstruction and the Fall of Paul de Man* (New York: Poseidon, 1991), pp. 143, 233.

48. Keys, *Post-Truth Era.*

49. Quoted in Nadya Labi, "When Teachers Cheat," *Time,* December 20, 1999.

50. Charlotte Allen, "Their Cheatin' Hearts," *Wall Street Journal,* May 11, 2007.

CHAPTER 5

1. Bill Zweicker, "Hot Rumors Dog Clintons," *Chicago Sun-Times,* February 19, 1993, and Roger Simon, "Hillary's Displeasure: Did Bill Urn It?" *Baltimore Sun,* March 29, 1993.

2. General Social Survey, Cumulative Datafile.

3. Peter Jennings, ABC Radio commentary, November 14, 1994.

4. *Washington Post,* April 25, 1995; Richard Lacayo, *Time* magazine; and Bryant Gumbel, *Today,* April 25, 1995. All quotes courtesy of the Media Research Center.

5. Quoted in Jonah Goldberg, "What's Not Right: How Democrats Use Rush Limbaugh," *National Review*, December 23, 2002.

6. John McCaslin, "Rabid Fox," *Washington Times*, April 11, 2005.

7. Bonnie Berry, *Social Rage: Emotion and Cultural Conflict* (New York: Garland, 1999).

8. David Morris, "Conservative Rage vs. Liberal Guilt," *Social Policy* (spring 2001).

9. Paul Starobin, "The Angry American," *Atlantic Monthly*, February 2004.

10. Michelle Malkin, *Unhinged: Exposing Liberals Gone Wild* (Washington, DC: Regnery, 2005), p. 164.

11. Kristin V. Jones, "Who Let the Punks Out? The Young and Angry Mosh Pit Vote for the November Election," *The Nation*, June 7, 2004.

12. Sarah Vowell, *Assassination Vacation* (New York: Simon & Schuster, 2005), pp. 7, 8.

13. Sam Worley-Ekstrom, "No More Liberal Compromises," *Mac Weekly*, February 6, 2004.

14. Gary Alan Fine, "Ire to the Chief," *Washington Post*, August 6, 2004.

15. General Social Survey, Cumulative Datafile.

16. Ibid.

17. Ibid.

18. Ibid.

19. Michael Lind, "Looking Back, Looking Forward," *The Nation*, December 20, 2004.

20. The Barna Group survey of 1,003 adults, October 2006.

21. George Varga, "The Real Deal," *San Diego Union-Tribune*, July 15, 2004.

22. Howard Kurtz, "A Dislike Unlike Any Other," *Washington Post*, October 19, 2003.

23. Simon Hattenstone, "Guerrilla in the Ritz," *The Guardian*, November 14, 2002.

24. Michelle Goldberg, "New York Lockdown," *Z Magazine*, August 12, 2004.

25. Casey Ross and Laurel Sweet, "Police Take a Bow for Safe DNC, Citywide Drop in Violent Crime," *Boston Herald*, July 31, 2004.

26. Michael Unger, *Newsday*, June 18, 2005.

27. Allen Ginsberg, interview with Matthew Rothschild, *The Progressive*, August 1994.

28. Richard Goldstein, "All the Rage," *Village Voice*, August 10, 1999.

29. "Envisioning the Future: Gloria Steinem," *Off Our Backs*, June 2000.

30. Kate Storm, "Fearless Rage; Powerful Feminist Audre Lorde Remembered on Her Birthday," *Eugene Weekly*, February 19, 2004.

31. "In Defense of Anger," *Earth First Journal,* April 30, 2004.

32. Rachel Neumann and David Glenn, "A Place for Rage," *Dissent* (spring 2000).

33. Michiko Kakatuni, "The Strange Case of the Writer and the Criminal," *New York Times,* September 20, 1981.

34. Clarence Page, "Black Rage May Be Real but No Rationale for Murder," *Rocky Mountain News,* June 23, 1994.

35. Remer Tyson, "Inward Rage; Young Finds Seething Frustration in Black Community," *Detroit Free Press,* July 19, 1987.

36. Eldridge Cleaver, *Soul on Ice* (New York: McGraw-Hill, 1967).

37. Cornel West, "On Black Rage," *Village Voice,* September 17, 1991.

38. Dan Lynch, "The Rage in Our Midst," *Atlanta Journal-Constitution,* April 5, 1994.

39. Introduction to Frantz Fanon, *Wretched of the Earth* (New York: Grove Press, 1965).

40. Quoted in E. J. Dionne, "We'll Get Over It If You Get Off Your High Horse," *Washington Post,* January 28, 2001.

41. Ann Marlowe, "Rage to Live," *Village Voice,* January 18, 1994.

42. Quoted in Peter Wood, *A Bee in the Mouth: Anger in America Now* (New York: Encounter, 2006), p. 99.

43. Paul Starobin, "The Angry American," *Atlantic Monthly*, January–February 2004.

44. Joe Klein, "Anger Management 101," *Time*, December 13, 2003.

45. Byron York, "Republicans Love It When Gore Gets Mad," *National Review Online*, May 27, 2004.

46. Glenn Thrush, "Clinton Says Criticism of Temper Is Sexism," *Newsday*, March 7, 2006.

47. Helen Dewar and Dana Milbank, "Cheney Dismisses Critic with Obscenity," Washingtonpost.com, June 25, 2004.

48. Cathy Burke, "Stormy Governor Spitzer's All the Rage," *New York Post*, July 15, 2007.

CHAPTER 6

1. George McGovern, *The Essential America: Our Founders and the Liberal Tradition* (New York: Simon & Schuster, 2004).

2. Brian C. Anderson, "Why Liberals Can't Keep Air America from Spiraling," *Los Angeles Times*, April 18, 2005.

3. Turner quoted in Robert Stacey McCain, *Washington Times*, February 17, 1999; Paul Begala, *The American Prospect*, October 16, 2001; Mark Morford, "When

Liberals Rule the World," *San Francisco Chronicle,* March 28, 2007.

4. Greg James, "First Person: Looking for Liberals? Follow Brains," *Seattle Post-Intelligencer,* August 25, 2003.

5. Alan Fram, "Book Chief: Conservatives Want Slogans," Associated Press, August 21, 2007.

6. Drew Westen, *The Political Brain: The Role of Emotion in Deciding the Fate of the Nation* (New York: Public Affairs, 2007).

7. Thomas Frank, *What's the Matter with Kansas?* (New York: Holt, 2005).

8. Norman Mailer, *The Big Empty: Dialogues on Politics, God, Sex, Boxing, Morality, Myth, Poker and Bad Conscience in America* (New York: Nation Books, 2006).

9. James Wolcott, "Red State Babylon," *Vanity Fair,* November 2006.

10. Denise Gellene, "Study Finds Left-Wing Brain, Right-Wing Brain," *Los Angeles Times,* September 10, 2007; ABC Radio Online, "AM—Study Finds Brain Differences Affect Political Views," September 10, 2007; "Left Brain, Right Brain," *Los Angeles Times,* September 12, 2007; William Saletin, "Liberal Interpretation: Rigging a Study to Make Conservatives Look Stupid," *Salon,* September 14, 2007.

11. Quoted in Cindy Yee, "DCU Sparks Various Reactions," *Duke Chronicle,* February 10, 2004.

12. Michael Berube, *What's Liberal about the Liberal Arts? Classroom Politics and 'Bias' in Higher Education* (New York: Norton, 2006).

13. Ibid.

14. "Too Stupid to Teach?" *Las Vegas Review-Journal,* March 23, 2004.

15. Quoted in Jonah Goldberg, "BullKrug," *National Review Online,* April 5, 2005.

16. For some examples of this, see Jennifer Braceras, "Gore's Dubious School Record," *Boston Globe,* September 7, 2000; Bill Nichols, "The Heir Apparent Has Solid Record and Stolid Image," *USA Today,* August 29, 1996; Richard Berke and Janet Elder, "The 2000 Campaign: The Poll; in Final Days, Voters Still Wrestle with Doubts on Bush and Gore," *New York Times,* October 23, 2000; Ross G. Brown, "Voting: Beating Up Smarty Pants," *Los Angeles Times,* October 28, 2000; and Jonathan Capehart, "Next Gore-Bush Debate Might Turn Nasty Again," Bloomberg News, October 9, 2000.

17. David Maraniss and Ellen Nakashima, "Gore's Grades Belie Image of Studiousness; His School Transcripts Are a Lot Like Bush's," *Washington Post,* March 19, 2000.

18. Howell Raines, "The 'Dumb' Factor," *Washington Post,* August 2, 2004.

19. John Tierney, "Political Points: Secret Weapon for Bush?" *New York Times,* October 24, 2004.

20. Geoff Kabaservice, "Bill Bradley's SAT Scores," *Slate,* January 26, 2000.

21. See http://lovenstein.org/report/.

22. See, for example, http://www.dailykos.com/story/2004/5/4/171620/3258.

23. "Clueless in St. James," *The Economist,* May 20, 2004.

24. William D. McIntosh, Rebecca M. Murray, John D. Murray, and Debra Sabia, "Are the Liberal Good in Hollywood?: Characteristics of Political Figures in Popular Films from 1945 to 1988," *Communication Reports,* vol. 16, no. 1 (2003).

25. Bill Maher, ABC, *Politically Incorrect,* February 6, 2001.

26. Bruce Fleming, *Why Liberals and Conservatives Clash* (New York: Routledge, 2006).

27. Emily Pronin, Justin Kruger, Kenneth Savitsky, and Lee Ross, "You Don't Know Me, But I Know You: The Illusion of Asymmetric Insight," *Journal of Personality and Social Psychology,* vol. 81, no. 4 (2001).

28. 2000 American National Election Study datafile.

29. 2004 American National Election Study datafile.

30. Social Capital Survey datafile.

31. Peter D. Hart Research Associates, Inc., A Survey of Attitudes Toward the American Judicial System, July 1986.

32. American National Election Study, Cumulative Datafile.

33. 1996 American National Election Study, using the variables v961006 ("Does respondent recall names of con-

gressional candidates?") and variable v961159 ("How often does respondent listen to Rush Limbaugh?").

34. C. Richard Hofstetter and Christopher L. Gianos, "Political Talk Radio: Actions Speak Louder Than Words," *Journal of Broadcasting and Electronic Media,* vol. 41, no. 4 (1997).

35. See Volokh.com.

36. Pew Research Center for People and the Press, *Generation Next Survey,* September 2006.

37. Kenneth Godwin, Jennifer Godwin, Valerie Martinez-Ebers, "Civic Socialization in Public and Fundamentalist Schools," *Social Science Quarterly,* vol. 85, no. 5 (December 2004).

38. 2000 American National Election Study datafile.

39. General Social Survey, Cumulative Datafile.

40. Ibid.

41. Alan S. Blinder and Alan B. Krueger, "What Does the Public Know About Economic Policy, and How Does It Know It?" Brookings Papers on Economic Activity, vol. 1 (2004).

42. Michael Weisskopf, *Washington Post,* February 1, 1993; Andy Rooney, quoted in Cal Thomas, "Anti-Christian Bias Characterizes CBS," syndicated column, November 25, 2004; and Kristof, quoted in Patrick Hynes, *In Defense of the Religious Right* (Nashville, TN: Nelson Current, 2006).

43. Chris Hedges, *American Fascists: The Christian Right and the War on America* (New York: Free Press, 2006).

44. Tom Purcell, "Politics of the Paranormal," *Pittsburgh Tribune-Review,* October 30, 2005; CBS News opinion poll, April 2002.

45. "What New Jerseyans Believe," *Star-Ledger/*Eagleton-Rutgers poll, Eagleton Institute of Politics, Rutgers University, April 9, 2000.

46. Francis Wheen, *Idiot Proof* (New York: Public Affairs, 2004), p. 120.

47. Robert McFadden, "Leading Americans Backed Jones Sect," *New York Times,* November 21, 1978.

48. Jonathan Chait, "Fact Finders," *New Republic,* February 22, 2005.

49. Dan Ackman and Elaine S. Povich, "President Hillary Clinton?" Forbes.com, September 6, 2006.

50. Wendy Kaminer, *Sleeping with Extra-Terrestrials: The Rise of Irrationalism and the Perils of Piety* (New York: Vintage, 1999), p. 166.

51. The Hotline, blog of the *National Journal,* October 3, 2005; Ian Bishop, *New York Post,* October 3, 2005.

52. Wheen, *Idiot Proof,* pp. 52–53.

53. James Atlas, "Erudite and Groovy," *New York Times,* August 7, 2000.

54. "Everyone Should See 'Inconvenient Truth,'" *Danbury News-Times,* June 27, 2006.

55. Norman Mailer, "The Search for Carter," *New York Times Magazine*, September 26, 1976.

56. Robert Sheaffer, "Jimmy Carter Reported a UFO Sighting While Governor of Georgia, Was in Fact the Planet Venus," *The Humanist*, July–August 1977, p. 46.

57. Shelley Ross, "Governor Carter's Wife: 'Jimmy and I Lived in a Haunted House for Five Years,' " *National Enquirer*, April 27, 1976.

CHAPTER 7

1. George Stephanopoulos, *All Too Human: A Political Education* (Boston: Little, Brown, 1999).

2. Quoted in Bob Woodward, *The Choice* (New York: Simon & Schuster, 1996).

3. Ralph Keyes, *The Post-Truth Era* (New York: St. Martin's Press, 2004), p. 84.

4. Andrew Ferguson, "Presidential Whining," *Time*, February 17, 1997.

5. *Lucas v. Saint Mary's Medical Center*, State of Wisconsin Department of Industry, Labor and Human Relations, Equal Rights Division, July 12, 1991, ERD Case Number 9051034.

6. Kenneth Minogue, *The Liberal Mind* (Liberty Fund reprint, 1963 edition).

7. Michael Crowley, "Former Senator Max Cleland: How the Disabled War Veteran Became the Democrats' Mascot," *Slate*, April 2, 2004.

8. Wendy Kaminer, "My Reputation: A Liberal Reflects on the Perils of Holding Modulated Views," *Atlantic Monthly*, October 1995.

9. Steven F. Hayward, "Killer Conservatives," *American Enterprise*, January 1, 2003.

10. Multi Investigator Study, 1998–99, variables wrla ("How satisfied with life these days") and variables cons for conservative and lib for liberals.

11. American National Election Study, Cumulative Datafile.

12. World Values Survey, Cumulative Datafile.

13. General Social Survey, Cumulative Datafile.

14. Ibid.

15. Bram P. Buunk et al., "The Division of Labor among Egalitarian and Traditional Women: Differences in Discontent, Social Comparison, and False Consensus," *Journal of Applied Psychology*, no. 30 (2000).

16. General Social Survey, Cumulative Datafile.

17. Social Capital Survey with variables HEALTH for "reported overall health" and IDEO for "self-reported political ideology."

18. General Social Survey, Cumulative Datafile.

19. Ibid.

20. Ibid.

21. Gregg Easterbrook, *The Progress Paradox* (New York: Random House, 2003), pp. 182–85.

22. Richard Dawkins, *River Out of Eden* (New York: Basic Books, 1995), and Jessica Matthews, "Evolution and Creationism," *Washington Post,* April 12, 1996.

23. Easterbrook, *Progress Paradox.*

24. With similar inaccuracy, the Club of Rome issued a study in 1972 announcing that the world would run out of gold by 1981, mercury by 1985, tin by 1987, zinc by 1990, oil by 1992, and copper by 1993.

25. Al Gore, *Earth in the Balance: Ecology and the Human Spirit* (Boston: Houghton Mifflin, 2000), p. 2.

26. Gerald Carbone, "Turner Urges Students to Save the World," *Providence Journal,* February 12, 2002, and Ken Auletta, "The Lost Tycoon," *New Yorker,* April 23, 2001.

27. See Robert P. George, *The Clash of Orthodoxies: Law, Religion, and Morality in Crisis* (Wilmington, DE: ISI Books, 2001).

28. See Anne Hendershott, *The Politics of Deviance* (New York: Encounter Books, 2002).

29. Quoted in Roger Kimball, *The Long March* (New York: Encounter Books, 2000).

30. General Social Survey, Cumulative Datafile.

31. Ibid.

32. Steven Stack and Ira Wasserman, "The Effects of Marriage, Family, and Religious Ties on African American Suicide Ideology," *Journal of Marriage and Family*, vol. 57, no. 1 (February 1995).

33. Steven Stack, "Gender, Marriage, and Suicide Acceptability: A Comparative Analysis," *Sex Roles: A Journal of Research*, vol. 38, no. 7–8 (1998).

34. Kanita Dervic, Maria A. Oquendo, Michael F. Grunebaum, Steve Ellis, Ainsley Burke, and J. John Mann, "Religious Affiliation and Suicide Attempt," *American Journal of Psychiatry* (December 2004).

35. Mike Wilson, "There Is Nothing Funny about the Clown Prince's Death," *Miami Herald*, April 22, 1989.

36. David Kupfer, interview with Paul Krasner, *The Progressive*, November 1993.

37. Lewis S. Feuer, "Some Irrational Sources of Opposition to the Market System," in Ernest van den Haag, ed., *Capitalism: Sources of Hostility* (New Rochelle, NY: Epoch Books, 1979).

38. Megan Dowd, "Canada Awaits American Influx," Fox News, January 20, 2005.

39. Ann Schroeder, "Names and Faces," *Washington Post*, November 12, 2004.

40. George Varga, "The Real Deal," *San Diego Union-Tribune*, July 15, 2004.

41. Jacquielynn Floyd, "Keillor's Dallas Jabs Read like Fictional Tale," *Dallas Morning News,* October 4, 2006.

42. Garrison Keillor, *Homegrown Democrat: A Few Plain Thoughts from the Heart of America* (New York: Penguin, 2006), p. 31.

43. Charles Krauthammer, "Where to Point Fingers," *Washington Post,* September 9, 2005.

44. Bruce Nolan, "Coalition Hears Katrina Testimony—Roles of Race, Class Explored in Inquiry," *New Orleans Times-Picayune,* June 30, 2006.

45. Cory Tolbert Haik and T. J. Ortenzi, "Rainbow PUSH Asks 'Recovery for Who?' " Nola.com, April 3, 2007.

46. Guy Taylor, "Barbau Steers Mississippi Toward Recovery," Washington Times, September 21, 2005.

CONCLUSION

1. Peter Berkowitz, "Introduction," Peter Berkowitz, ed., *Never a Matter of Indifference: Sustaining Virtue in a Free Republic* (Stanford, CA: Hoover Institution Press, 2003).

INDEX

Abzug, Bella, 12, 146, 176
academics, 13, 19, 75, 167
  conservatives attacked and
    stereotyped by, 2–5, 15, 137,
    141, 160, 209
  dishonesty of, 128–31
  work ethic dismissed by, 92
  see also universities
Affluent Society, The (Galbraith), 195
Alinsky, Saul, 115–16, 125
American Enterprise Institute,
  150–51, 188
*American Journal of Drug and
  Alcohol Abuse,* 53
American Journal of Psychiatry, 200
American National Election Survey,
  69, 161–62, 169–70, 188–89
American Political Science Review, 12
American Psychological Association,
  4, 193
American Scholar, 38

Anderson, Brian, 15
Anti-Intellectualism in American Life
  (Hofstadter), 12
anti-Semitism, 19–20
Arkansas Gazette, 153
Ashcroft, John, 176–77
Assassination Vacation (Vowell), 140

Bailey, F. G., 128
Baker, Nicholson, 139–40
Baltimore Sun, 133
Barone, Michael, 96
Barry, Dave, 11
Bateson, Mary Catherine, 178
Bee in the Mouth, A (Wood), 139
Begala, Paul, 9, 158
Bender, Thomas, 128
Berkeley, University of California at,
  2, 3, 4, 5, 21, 61, 74, 201
Berkowitz, Peter, 212

Berry, Bonnie, 138
Berube, Michael, 161
Biden, Joe, 117
Big Empty, The (Mailer), 159
blacks, 27, 35, 149–50
Blinder, Alan S., 173
Bloom, Allan, 105–6
Bloom, Marshall, 201
blue states, 9, 10, 33, 75, 159
Bond, Julian, 150
Bonjour Laziness (Maier), 91
Bork, Robert, 24, 54
Boston Globe, 165
Boston Phoenix, 138–39
Boteach, Shmuley, 39
Boxer, Barbara, 8
Bradley, Bill, 165
Bradley, Ed, 50
Brandon, Robert, 160–61
Brooks, Arthur, 57, 70
Brooks, David, 25
Brooks, Renana, 202
Brown, Willie, 118
Brummett, John, 153
Buchanan, Pat, 118, 138, 151
Bush, George H. W., 151, 163, 166, 203
Bush, George W., 10, 11, 12, 13, 17, 63–64, 68, 75, 85, 99, 127, 138, 139–41, 144, 145, 146, 151, 152, 154, 159, 161, 162–63, 165, 166, 173, 174, 176, 180, 185, 186, 188, 201, 205–6
Bush Survival Bible (Stone), 202

Caldicott, Helen, 197
Camelot and the Cultural Revolution (Piereson), 13–14

Caputo, Bruce, 117
Carter, Jimmy, 29, 57, 166, 180, 196
Carter, Stephen, 132
"Case Against Kids, The," 38
"Case for Bush Hatred, The," 139
Castro, Fidel, 4, 82
Catalogue for Philanthropy, The, 75
Celestine Prophecy, The (Redfield), 177
Center for Democracy and Citizenshp, 76
Center for Survey Research & Analysis, 5
Chait, Jonathan, 139, 144
Charlotte, N.C., 75
Chase, Leah, 207
Checkpoint (Baker), 139–40
Cheney, Dick, 63, 64, 150, 151, 154, 169, 184
Chicago Sun-Times, 3, 10, 133
Chicago Tribune, 204
children, 68
    conservatives and, 2, 20, 32, 35, 44–45
    conservatives as, 2, 3
    drug abuse by, 52–53
    illegitimate, 10–11
    liberals and, 20, 31–46
    liberals as, 2, 3, 8
Chomsky, Noam, 92
Chopra, Deepak, 177–78
Christian Science Monitor, 74
Church of the Movement of Inner Spiritual Awareness, 73
Clausen, Christopher, 38
Clinton, Bill, 9, 30, 40, 48, 63, 76, 81–82, 85, 99, 113, 116, 117–18, 119–22, 135, 152–54, 166, 178–80, 183–87, 203

Clinton, Hillary, 35, 44, 46, 56, 57,
  63, 81–82, 83, 101, 115, 116,
  133–34, 152, 153, 177–79, 183,
  184–85
Clinton administration, 5, 52, 60, 86,
  92, 125, 173, 177
Closing of the American Mind, The
  (Bloom), 105–6
Coffin, Tom, 51–52
Congress, U.S., 64, 118, 134, 178
  see also House of Representatives,
  U.S.; Senate, U.S.
Conscience of a Liberal (Wellstone),
  39–40
conservatives:
  charity practiced by, 55–79
  "compassionate," 86
  differences between liberals and
  (overview), 15–27
  family relationships and, 2, 3,
  20–21, 36, 42, 43–45
  honesty valued by, 105–32
  as less money-centered than
  liberals, 81–104
  as less self-centered than liberals,
  29–54
  liberal disparagement of, 1–27,
  56–57, 61, 71–72, 85–86,
  137–41, 152–54, 157–68, 209
  as "makers," 26–27
  media misrepresentation of, 4, 5–7,
  86, 134–37, 158, 162–63
  personality and moral traits of,
  23–24, 76–77, 137, 209–12
  religious, 41, 47, 70
  selfishness ascribed to, 3
  superior knowledge of, 157–81
  whining avoided by, 183–208
  work ethic supported by, 90–104

see also radio talk shows; red
  states; Republicans, Republican
  Party
Conservatives Without a Conscience
  (Dean), 6
Coulter, Ann, 138
Countdown, 7
Craig, Larry, 119
Crane, Dan, 118–19
Cuomo, Andrew, 56, 57–58
Cuomo, Mario, 40, 150, 154, 157

Daily Kos, 6, 33, 61, 137
Daily Show, The, 7, 37
Dawkins, Richard, 194
Dean, Howard, 3, 8–9, 143,
  152–53
Dean, John, 6–7
de Man, Paul, 129–30
Democratic Leadership Council, 58,
  152
Democratic National Committee
  (DNC), 3, 153
Democratic National Conventions,
  40, 62, 122–23, 145
Democrats, Democratic Party, 1, 2, 3,
  8, 11, 20, 27, 53, 61, 65, 69–70,
  73–74, 76, 89, 93, 99, 111, 158,
  160, 164, 166, 170, 171–73,
  187, 188, 190–91, 202
Dionne, E. J., 151
Dissent, 147
Dole, Bob, 76
Douglas, Michael, 136
drugs, 48–53, 77
Ducat, Stephen, 6
Duke University, 87, 131, 160, 172
Dworkin, Ronald, 104, 199

Early, David, 11
Easterbrook, Gregg, 195
economists:
  free market, 24
  laissez-faire, 78
  liberal, 5
  social power of, 24–25
  "trickle-down," 86
Edelman, Peter, 92
education, 35, 91–92, 131–32, 160,
  171, 172
  see also universities
Edwards, John, 64, 83–84, 90, 92,
  101, 150
Ehrlich, Paul, 195–96
elections, U.S.:
  of 1960, 203
  of 1964, 13, 185
  of 1992, 203
  of 1994, 134, 178
  of 1996, 76, 203
  of 2000, 137, 152, 162, 169, 171,
    201
  of 2004, 3, 10, 14, 75, 138, 139,
    143, 152–53, 163–65, 169, 174,
    201, 203–4
  of 2006, 61
environmental issues, 12, 77, 145,
  147, 195–98
Envy (Schoeck), 103–4

Fact, 13
Falling Down, 136
Fanatics and Fools (Huffington),
  72–73
Feinstein, Dianne, 150
feminism, feminists, 37–38, 42, 147,
  150, 191, 200

Fine, Gary Alan, 141
Fitzsimmons, Ron, 126
Fleming, Bruce, 18, 76–77, 168
Foley, Mark, 119
Forbes, 177
Fourier, Charles, 36
Frank, Thomas, 158–59
Franken, Al, 49, 135, 137, 143–44
Frost, Adrianne, 37

Galbraith, John Kenneth, 5, 85,
  195
General Social Survey, 19–20, 30–33,
  36, 47, 70, 88, 97–98, 114, 134,
  141, 142–43, 172, 189–90, 192,
  200
Gephardt, Richard, 90, 121, 152
Get to Work (Hirshman), 38–39
Gibson, Charlie, 86
Gingrich, Newt, 118
Ginsberg, Allen, 146
Gitlin, Todd, 147
Glenn, David, 147–48
Goldstein, Richard, 147
Goldwater, Barry, 13, 101–2,
  185
Good Morning America, 86
Gore, Al, 58–59, 99, 122–24, 152,
  162–63, 169, 179, 185, 188,
  198
Gotti, John, 122
Greater Good Science Center, 92
Great Speckled Bird, 51
Greenwald, Glenn, 151
Greer, Evelyn, 131
Guardian, 145, 160
Guevara, Che, 95
Gumbel, Bryant, 84, 135

Habitat for Humanity, 68
Haitian Health Foundation, 68
Hannity, Sean, 143, 203
Harvard, 74, 85
Harvard University, 5, 40, 57, 74, 163
Hayward, Stephen, 188
Herskovitz, Marshall, 121
Hirshman, Linda, 37, 38–39
Hoffman, Abbie, 50–51, 146, 200–201
Hofstadter, Richard, 12, 13
Holmes, Oliver Wendell, 104
Homegrown Democrat (Keillor), 204
Hook, Sidney, 106
House of Representatives, U.S., 116, 119, 170
Houston, Jean, 178
Huffington, Arianna, 72–73
Hume, Edward, 197
Humphrey, Hubert, 29
Hunt, Al, 60
Hymowitz, Kay, 40

I Hate Other People's Kids (Frost), 37
Inconvenient Truth, An, 179
Institute for America's Future, 66
Integrity (Carter), 132
Internal Revenue Service (IRS), 64, 67, 68, 72, 75, 85, 108–9
see also taxes
Internet, 5, 39, 84, 86
see also websites, liberal
Investor's Business Daily, 153
IQ, 166–67
Ivins, Molly, 90

Jackson, Jesse, 71–72, 207–8
Jefferson, William, 207
Jelen, Ted, 161
Jerusalem Center for Public Affairs, 19
Jews, 19–29, 107, 169
JFK, 124–25
Journal of Adolescent Health, 45
Journal of Business Ethics, 110, 112–13
Journal of Management Development, 98
Journal of Psychology, 111–12
Journal of Research in Personality, 3
Journal of Social Psychology, 94

Kaminer, Wendy, 48, 187–88
Katrina, Hurricane, 206–8
Kaul, Donald, 118
Keillor, Garrison, 8, 56–57, 67, 69, 203–6
Kennedy, Edward, 60, 63
Kennedy, John F., 14, 29, 63, 124–25, 166, 184, 203, 211
Kerry, John, 3, 10, 50, 59–60, 75, 99, 139, 152, 163–65, 202–3
Keynes, John Maynard, 24–25
Kinsley, Michael, 11
Kirk, Grayson, 14
Klein, Jonathan, 137
Kohn, Alfie, 91–92
Koppel, Ted, 126
Kotkin, Joel, 32
Kristof, Nicholas, 174
Kristol, Bill, 138
Kristol, Irving, 24
Krugman, Paul, 140, 176

Lacayo, Richard, 135
Lakoff, George, 2–3, 20
Lamont, Ned, 61–62
Laura Ingraham Show, 143
Lawrence, Larry, 117–18
Leach, Edmund, 36
Leahy, Patrick, 154
Lehane, Chris, 59
Leiter, Brian, 161
Leukemia & Lymphoma Society, 68
Levy, Bob, 117
Lewis, Anthony, 85
Liberal Mind, The (Minogue),
 186–87
liberals:
 anger and, 133–55, 210
 archetypes and icons of, 29, 62,
  146, 148–49, 211
 charity avoided by, 55–79
 conservatives rebuked and
  caricatured by, 1–27, 56–57, 61,
  71–72, 85–86, 137–41, 152–54,
  157–68, 209
 differences between conservatives
  and, summarized, 15–27
 family relationships and, 2, 3, 8,
  31–46
 honesty not valued by, 105–32
 "instant rich," 97
 knowledge limitations of, 157–81
 money envy and obsession of,
  81–104
 personality and moral traits of,
  21–32, 76–77, 209–12
 self-centeredness of, 29–54
 self-image of, 2–3, 7–8, 14, 57, 72,
  79, 155, 168
 as "takers," 27
 "trust fund," 96–97

whining by, 21, 183–208
work ethic eschewed by, 24,
 90–104
see also academics; blue states;
 Democrats, Democratic Party
Lieberman, Joe, 61, 152, 169
Limbaugh, Rush, 4, 65, 68, 118, 170
Lind, Michael, 142
Lindgren, James, 78, 103
Livingston, Bob, 122
Locked in the Cabinet (Reich), 125
Lorde, Audre, 147
Los Angeles Times, 6, 8, 160, 202
Lovenstein Institute, 166
Luks, Samantha, 87

Madison, University of Wisconsin at,
 116
Maher, Bill, 19, 49, 136
Maier, Corinne, 91
Mailer, Norman, 148, 159, 180
Malthus, Thomas, 90
Marine Corps–Law Enforcement
 Foundation, 68
Marlowe, Ann, 150
Marriage of Sense and Soul, The, 179
Marx, Groucho, 1
Marx, Karl, 78, 95, 111
Marxists, 14, 95, 159
Matthews, Jessica, 194–95
McAuliffe, Terry, 153
McCurry, Mike, 48
McGovern, George, 50, 157
McKinley, William, 140, 184
Medeiros, Gia, 178
media, 153, 183
 conservatives as viewed by, 4, 5–7,
  86, 134–37, 158, 162–63

positive aspects of conservatives
　ignored by, 19, 57
see also radio talk shows
Media Matters, 66
Menchu, Rigoberta, 130
Michael Medved Show, 143
Miller, Stephen, 150–51
"Mind of Barry Goldwater, The"
　(Ginsberg), 13
Minogue, Kenneth, 186–87
Mirels-Garrett Protestant Work Ethic
　Scale, 94
Mollen, Debra, 38
Mondale, Walter, 176
money:
　liberal attitude toward, 81–104
Moore, Michael, 66–67, 83, 90–91,
　92, 138, 144–45, 167–68, 201,
　203
Moral Politics (Lakoff), 2–3
Morrison, Toni, 37
Moser, John, 161
Moulitsas, Markos, 137
Moving Beyond Words (Steinem), 147
Moyers, Bill, 12, 199
Muravchik, Joshua, 107
Musselman, Elaine, 116
My Cold War (Kristol), 24
My Life (Clinton), 30
My Name Is Barbra, 66

Nader, Ralph, 71, 144
Nation, 127, 139, 142
National Center for Health Statistics,
　33
National Cultural Values Survey, 107,
　112, 114
National Institutes of Health, 38

National Opinion Research Center,
　20
National Survey of Families and
　Households, 44–45
Nation of Victims, A (Sykes), 187
Neumann, Rachel, 147–48
New Age movement, 47–48, 73, 176,
　177, 178–79
New Republic, 137, 139, 144, 176
Newsweek, 35, 135–36
New York, 13, 154, 185
New Yorker, 46, 121
New York Observer, 92
New York Times, 5, 7, 12, 14, 50, 51,
　56, 57, 83, 85, 91, 92, 101, 140,
　148, 158, 163, 164, 174, 176,
　185
New York Times Book Review, 139–40
Nightline, 126

Obama, Barack, 64, 115
O'Donnell, Rosie, 84
Office of National Drug Control
　Policy, 52
Oklahoma City bombing, 135
Olbermann, Keith, 7
O'Neill, John, 144
One True Thing (Quindlen), 199
Oprah, 120
O'Reilly, Bill, 68
O'Rourke, William, 10
Owens, Major, 40

Page, Clarence, 149
Panzer, Mary, 116
PBS, 3, 49, 199
Pearson, Drew, 14

Pelosi, Nancy, 65–66, 67–68
Perle, Richard, 138
Pew Research Center, 93, 108, 172, 188
Pheiffer, Sherman, 202
Piereson, James, 13–14
"Politics of Family, The" (Kuttner), 6
Population Bomb (Ehrlich), 195–96
Prevalence of Deceit, The (Bailey), 128
Psychological Bulletin, 4
Psychology Today, 6
Publishers Weekly, 6
Pynchon, Thomas, 195

Quindlen, Anna, 199

Rader, Dennis, 137
radio talk shows, 4, 135, 146, 171
"Rage for Justice" awards, 150
Raines, Howell, 164
Rall, Ted, 12, 14
Rasmussen, Paul, 205
Rather, Dan, 127
Rauch, Jonathan, 125
Reagan, Ronald, 13, 24, 29–30, 51, 63, 86, 99, 125–26, 151, 154, 166, 176, 197
Real Time, 19
Red State, 9
red states, 9–12, 33, 75, 159
Reich, Robert, 5, 60–61, 84, 125
relativism, 24, 25, 106, 112–13, 115, 132, 137, 210
religion, 41, 47, 70, 174–77, 180
Republicans, Republican Party, 1, 4, 8–9, 11, 13, 20, 50, 53, 56, 65,

69–70, 76, 93, 99, 116–19, 122, 139, 145, 152, 159, 166, 171–73, 176, 184, 188, 190–91
Revolution from Within (Steinem), 37
Rhodes, Randi, 137
Rich, Frank, 12
Road to Wigan Pier, The (Orwell), 18
Robert Morris University, 102–3
Roberts, Steven, 134
Ronstadt, Linda, 144, 204
Roosevelt, Eleanor, 62, 179
Roosevelt, Franklin D., 29, 62–63, 211
Rossi, Alice, 37
Rowan, Carl, 135

Sagan, Carl, 197
Sahehan, Sam, 121
Said, Edward, 128–29
Salant, Richard, 127
San Francisco, Calif., 31, 32, 65, 68, 74–75, 110, 118, 119, 203
San Francisco Chronicle, 5, 6, 158
San Jose Mercury News, 11, 51
Sartre, Jean-Paul, 150, 195
Saturday Night Live, 49
Savio, Mario, 201
Schoeck, Helmut, 103–4
Schooler, Douglas, 202
Schroeder, Patricia, 158
Schumer, Chuck, 19
Schwab, Klaus, 179
Seattle Post-Intelligencer, 158
Seinfeld, 40
Seligman, Martin, 193–94

Senate, U.S., 61, 154, 163, 170,
176–77, 178
Seven Spiritual Laws of Success, The
(Chopra), 177–78
Sewell, Sam, 165
Sex Roles, 200
Shaw, George Bernard, 95–96
Sherkat, Darren, 34–35
60 Minutes, 127, 174
Slouching Toward Gomorrah (Bork),
24
Smiley, Jane, 11–12, 121, 139
Smith, Kevin, 9
Smith College, 40, 68
Snyder, Mitch, 125–26
Social Capital Community
Benchmark Survey, 74–75
Social Capital Survey, 169, 190, 191
Social Policy, 138
Social Rage (Berry), 138
Social Security, 32, 173, 185
Soros, George, 77, 85, 107
Soviet Union, 14, 197
Sowell, Thomas, 208
Spitzer, Eliot, 154
Spock, Benjamin, 92
Stack, Steve, 199, 200
Stand Up and Fight Back (Dionne),
151
Stanford University, 4, 162, 168
Starobin, Paul, 151
Starobin, Robert, 201
Steal This Movie, 51
Steinem, Gloria, 37, 42, 146, 147
Stenner, Karen, 5
Stephanopoulos, George, 183
Stewart, Jon, 7
Stoll, David, 130
Stone, Gene, 202

Stone, Oliver, 124–25
Strategic Petroleum Reserve, 122
Streisand, Barbra, 66
Studds, Gerry, 119
Supreme Court, U.S., 111, 169–70,
199
Sutton, Robert, 131–32
Switzler, Royall, 117
Sykes, Charles, 187

taxes, 24, 40, 62, 64, 66, 67, 73, 77,
84, 85, 96, 107–8, 109, 173
Tedisco, James, 154
Thatcher, Margaret, 77–78
Theory of Everything, A (Wilber),
180
Think Progress, 6
Thomas, Evan, 135
Thompson, Hunter S., 49–50
Thornhill, Randy, 42
Time, 36, 135, 185–86, 194
Time to Run, A (Boxer), 8
Today, 135
Toronto Star, 3
Troupe, Quincy, 128
Trudeau, Garry, 166–67
Turner, Ted, 33, 82–83, 157–58,
198–99
Two Kinds (Weaver), 7

universities, 35
conservatives physically attacked
at, 138
liberal bias at, 5, 87, 160
see also academics
Urbanski, Douglas, 145
U.S. News & World Report, 5, 134

Vaillant, George, 73–74
Vanity Fair, 9, 30, 159
Village Voice, 91, 147
Volokh, Eugene, 171
volunteering, 68–69, 70–71, 75
von Hoffman, Nicholas, 92
Vonnegut, Kurt, 11
Vowell, Sarah, 140

Wallace, Chris, 185
Wall Street Journal, 60
Walters, Barbara, 133
Walton, Sam, 77
Warwick University, 102
Washington, Booker T., 208
Washington Monthly, 38
Washington Post, 57, 82, 135, 137,
    140, 151, 152–53, 174, 194
Wasserman, Ira, 200
Waters, Maxine, 150
Weaver, Jim, 7, 85–86
websites, liberal, 6, 167
Weinstein, Bob and Harvey, 145
Weisskopf, Michael, 174
welfare, 24, 92–93, 94, 107
Wellesley College, 56, 115, 130
Wellstone, Paul, 39–40

West, Cornel, 149
Westen, Drew, 158
What's the Matter with Kansas?
    (Frank), 158–59
Who Really Cares? (Brooks), 57
Wilber, Ken, 179–80
Wildavsky, Aaron, 186
Wilkins, Roy, 176
Willaerts, Adam, 59
Williamson, Marianne, 178
Wills, Garry, 13, 174
Wimp Factor, The (Ducat), 6
Wisconsin Department of Labor and
    Human Relations, 186
Wolcott, James, 9, 10, 136–37, 159
Wood, Peter, 139
work ethic, 24, 90–104
World Economic Forum (2006),
    179–80
World Trade Organization (WTO),
    145, 147
World Values Survey, 34, 41, 42, 88,
    89, 94, 106–7, 111, 112, 154,
    189

Yale University, 129, 163, 164